103 Ways To Earn Money As A Professional Writer

by
Scott Martin

Published by Scott Martin
2820 Selwyn Avenue
Suite 750
Charlotte NC 28209
www.scottmartincopywriter.com

SECOND EDITION Editor Christy Goldfeder

ISBN: 978-1-7373340-0-2 (Paperback)
ISBN: 978-1-7373340-1-9 (Ebook)

Book Interior and E-book Design by Amit Dey | amitdey2528@gmail.com

Dedication

To my fellow professional writers around the planet.

Table of Contents

Introduction

So You Want to Be a Writer?

I count myself as one of the most fortunate people on the planet. Yes—I'm fortunate to have a wonderful life outside my work but I'm especially lucky to be a professional writer.

Every major advance in technology has created exponential opportunities for writers. Sometime close to 1450, Johannes Gutenberg invented the printing press. Soon, printing presses were being produced by the thousands and this created a TON of work for writers. After all, someone had to write the books and printed materials that owners of the presses needed to print.

Fast forward several centuries to the late 1700s when newspapers became a big business...due to innovations in printing presses. The publishers needed to fill the pages with copy, and there was a big demand for journalists and editors. Newspapers included advertisements and writers had to create the ads.

At the end of the 19th century, big catalog companies like Sears took advantage of further advances in printing technology. The catalog companies each employed thousands of writers and editors to write pages and pages of catalog copy.

In the 20th century, radio created work for writers who had to write the radio shows. Then TV came along and, again, the producers of the TV shows needed writers to write scripts and create ideas. Most 30 minute TV shows included 6-7 minutes of commercials; writers had to write these commercials.

With the arrival and growth of the Internet, the opportunities for writers increased again. Think about it. In 1992, there were roughly 100 websites. Today, as I write, nobody really knows the number of websites, but Google estimates that there are around 9.4 billion as of January 2019.

Well, my writing brothers and sisters, someone has to write the content for all those pages and all those sites. Some website owners write their own copy. But many companies, as you'll discover, outsource the writing. Bigger companies pay writers to write website copy full-time.

And those crazy numbers above don't include emails and related print content. Think about the companies in the Fortune 500. Each company sends out thousands of unique emails a week...probably close to 100,000 different emails a year. So that's upwards of 50 million emails a year from just 500 companies. And someone has to write those emails.

Perhaps one day, someone with the ingenuity of a Johannes Gutenberg will create software that produces writing. I think we're a long way off from that...plus here's another problem for companies that's a huge opportunity for writers. You cannot duplicate content. One, it's illegal due to copyright laws. Two, Google punishes websites for using duplicate copy. And, at least in the online world, Google is judge and jury; I don't see the day coming when Google and the other search engines reward companies for plagiarism: this means there will always be a need for fresh content. And this means a steady stream of work for writers.

Writing is the foundation of the creative process, and I very much doubt a computer can ever be truly creative. Yes—a computer can beat me at chess (which is essentially a mathematical exercise) but a computer cannot replicate the creative process, in part, because the creative process is not mathematical and not always logical.

Technology Has Hurt Some Writers...But Helped Others

From 1995 to 2000, I worked for a big newspaper company. I was in a sales and management role. My job was to create new publications. I wasn't a journalist or editor, but I had a front row seat to the financial and professional disaster that took place, and is still taking place, in the newspaper industry.

Newspapers used to make big, fat margins: upwards of 30%. Today, for every dollar of revenue from the old print model, newspapers make 10 cents in the digital world. It's been carnage. And technology is to blame. The Internet has basically destroyed the financial stability of the newspaper industry and tens of thousands of journalists have been left without jobs. The writers who create a newspaper—journalists and editors—still exist but, as I describe in the chapter about being a journalist, it's not a great gig.

So…one goal of this book is to educate people who have been 'displaced' so they understand the alternatives. I used to be in the print world. I published a quarterly magazine. I moved into a different field, and I'm delighted with the change. I'm now a direct response copywriter. I also create information products—like this one.

Technology has also hurt the book publishing industry. About 10 years ago, authors had to work with an agent and/or a publishing house. Today, authors, as you'll discover, can publish their work in a variety of ways. So the editors in the publishing houses have been hit. Quite frankly, their somewhat dated business model needed some major changes anyway.

However, technology, specifically the Internet, has been especially valuable for:

- Copywriters
- Information publishers
- Authors
- Bloggers
- Content producers

You can discover more about these opportunities later in the book.

In this book, I provide a clear picture of the current writing landscape for professional writers. You get:

- A description of the actual writing work required.
- How to break into the field.
- What you can expect to earn.
- Street-smart advice including how to avoid the scum who do not pay very well.
- Additional information including links to associations, job boards, plus information to help you succeed in that field...where applicable.

Whether you're changing careers after several years in one field, or if you're a student looking for some career direction, you'll find this guide useful. It will help you make an educated decision.

Online Articles and Blogging

A t least three times a month, a writer will call or email and ask, "I really want to become a writer. What should I do?"

Here's my advice:

Learn how to blog. Learn to create and/or repurpose web content and articles.

With little or no experience writing content or blogging, you can quickly write 8-10 blogs or articles a day and get paid at least $50 for each article or blog. That's a potential gross income of $500 a day, which is $10,000 a week and well into 6-figure range. Even at the low end of the scale, you can easily earn $250 a day. That's a potential gross income of $60,000 and you can complete the work in your pajamas or smoking jacket. The choice is yours. No commuting. No office politics, etc. etc.

Once you build a portfolio of blogs, and if you enjoy the blogging experience, you can specialize in blogging. Some companies will pay close to $250 for a regular blog. I rarely work on other blogs today, but when I was building my copywriting business, blogs and articles provided a valuable and dependable income stream.

So, in this chapter, I'm going to detail why blogging and article writing are important to companies—and why companies pay for this content. I'm also going to provide all the other details about blogging and content.

In fact, I'm even going to introduce a way to make a significant sum each month from *your* blog.

The Value of Fresh Content

Content is a very broad term that covers everything from what appears on TV shows to the words in a book. In the world of blogging and articles, content is just that—blogs and articles.

A blog is short for a 'web log' or, to be more precise, a blog is a journal. In the United Kingdom, it's called a diary. It might be me but it seems that every website has a blog. I have a blog on my site (scottmartincopywriter. com/blog/). I have also written blogs for a company called Crazy Egg (crazyegg.com); the company provides software for web analytics.

Companies primarily use blogs for two reasons:

1. Communicate with their customers and employees.
2. Provide fresh content to the search engines.

Some companies take their blogging seriously and pay writers several hundred dollars per blog. Others simply have a blog to help with their rankings in the search engines. I won't dive too deeply into search engine marketing and how search engines work, but here's an important fact that every professional writer must understand.

Google and the search engines LOVE fresh content.

A blog provides the search engines with new words and gives the robots a feast. Search engines like Google send out these robots to scan websites find new content. When the robots find this fresh content, they report back to the 'mother' robot and search engine rankings—so vital to so many businesses—can improve. Again, I've provided a massively oversimplified version of how the search engines work.

As a writer, it's helpful to understand SEO basics but it's not vital to have a doctorate in the subject. However, I recommend you learn about keywords.

Keywords are words and phrases that people enter when they are searching for information. For example, when people are searching for a direct response copywriter, they will enter 'direct response copywriter' into a search engine. So my blog always includes the phrase 'direct response copywriter.' Google provides a free tool to help with keyword searches. (https://adwords.google.com/o/KeywordTool)

When you write a blog, the person giving you the assignment will often require that you include certain keywords in the blog. For example, let's say you're writing a weekly blog for a local veterinarian in Seattle. You'll want to include the words "Seattle vet" in the copy. But you'll need to be careful NOT to make the copy sound too contrived.

For several years, people would write stilted sentences like "There are many forms of Seattle vet in the Seattle vet landscape... and so it's important for Seattle vets to visit other Seattle vets to see what Seattle vets are up to." Google actually demotes sites, or bans them altogether, for including this type of contrived language.

For at least three years, I wrote a weekly blog post. These days, I write less frequently. But when I do publish, I include several keywords I know are powerful when it comes to search engine optimization, and I've steadily climbed the search rankings. My website organically generates quality leads.

Articles

To give their SEO rankings an even bigger boost, many companies create new web pages and populate the pages with articles. These read like newspaper articles. Again, to gain the most impact, it's important to include the keywords. The client will provide the keyword(s) they want included in the article.

OK—let's get down to the nitty-gritty.

What the Work Involves

Blogging. A company will contract you to write a blog... usually a series of blogs.

- You receive the idea or theme for the blog. Or you come up with ideas.
- You research the material or the client provides the material.

- Write the blog and include the keywords. A blog is usually around 500 words.
- Find images.
- Provide links to material you may have sourced.
- Review the copy with the client.
- Send the blog live.
- Review comments.

The process is somewhat similar with articles.

- You receive the idea or theme for the article. Or you come up with an idea.
- Research the material or the client will provide the material.
- Write the article and include the keywords. An article is usually around 500-1,000 words.
- A client may give you material they have already written but they want the copy rewritten so it's not seen as plagiarized.
- Find images (if applicable).
- Provide links to material you may have sourced.
- Review the copy with the client.
- Send the article live.

So...it's not overly complicated. If you're familiar with the subject matter, there's no need for complex research. The language can be simple and straightforward. In many cases, even if you're being paid for the article or blog, you can persuade the client to provide a link to your blog or, better still, your website: this provides a useful SEO advantage.

How to Get Started in Blogging and Articles

Nobody really knows how many blogs are currently being published. However, blogs provide 'newbie' professional writers with a tremendous opportunity to earn a decent income very quickly. When I was writing blogs and articles more frequently, I could write a simple blog in about 30 minutes and I would often receive $50 per blog. Run the numbers.

If you haven't written blogs or articles, write your own. Start by setting up your own blog on a blogging platform like:

- Blogger (blogger.com)
- Wordpress (wordpress.com)
- Medium (medium.com)
- Squarespace (squarespace.com - my favorite)
- Wix (wix.com)
- Weebly (weebly.com)
- Tumblr (tumblr.com)

There are hundreds of blogging platforms. Some are free but, to be taken seriously, it helps to have your personal custom domain. A site like Wordpress charges a small one time fee for a custom domain.

Blog every day so you build up a portfolio. In 30 days, you'll have plenty you can show to a prospective client. Make sure your blog is completely free of typos; hire a proofreader.

I have not used Blogger or Tumblr. I used to use Wordpress and it's a popular choice. I prefer Squarespace because it's easier—and I built my website on the platform. Many people like Wordpress for their entire website. Once you have established your blog and also written articles, you can build a website for your business around your blog.

Because there's a big demand for blogging and articles, there's a healthy market. Several websites list 'gigs' from companies all over the world. You can complete a Google search for "blogging jobs" or "article writing" for the most up-to-date listings.

Perhaps the three biggest and most powerful sites for finding freelance blogging work are:

- Upwork (https://www.upwork.com)

- BloggingPro (http://www.bloggingpro.com)
- Pro Blogger (http://jobs.problogger.net)
- Freelance Writing Gigs (http://www.freelancewritinggigs.com)

You can also look at local businesses (of any size) you admire and see if they have a blog. If they have one, they will likely prefer to outsource the task. The marketing manager or business owner usually looks at their blog as a chore and will consider outsourcing the work.

Find local SEO experts by completing a Google search. SEO experts (if they are really actual experts) should tell their clients to invest in a blog and fresh article content. Many SEO specialists are NOT writers and will refer you to their clients. Again—before you approach people, you need to have a blog and articles.

I think it's easy to come up with ideas and subjects for blogs and articles. If you're stuck, look at your local newspaper for the types of articles that are published. The ideas I like:

- "How to" pieces
- Something about current events
- Insider knowledge
- Success stories
- Current problems and how to overcome them
- Stories about people in a company or industry
- Latest innovations

Remember that blog and article content can be repurposed into case studies, newsletter articles, and even into a book. Recently, I finished ghost-writing a book for a client; I started with his blog content and much of the initial content came from his blog.

Earning Expectations

As I wrote earlier, blogging and article fees range from $5 per blog to several hundred dollars. You can also charge a monthly retainer for maintenance of a blog or providing a set number of articles. However, I believe even a mildly competent writer with even modest sales skills can make at least $60,000 a year writing blogs and content. Yes—it's a lot of typing but it's relatively easy work and there's a huge demand for fresh content.

How to Avoid the Scum... and Other Notes

Beware the evil 'content farmers' who pay around $5 an article and believe that's a fair way to pay writers. Two I've flirted with (briefly) are Copypress (www.copypress.com) and Demand Studios (http://www.demandstudios.com). You bid on the work (lowest price wins). Many of these businesses are no longer in around because Google changed its search results algorithm to punish these low-quality content sites.

You can find plenty of blogging work on crowdsourcing sites like upwork (www.upwork.com) but stick to finding people who have regular needs.

Check out local businesses to see if they have a blog. You can approach theses businesses with a monthly plan where the company pays anywhere from $100 to $300 a month for you to write and manage their blog. Once you explain the SEO benefits and the fact that a good blog can even help to sell their services/products, the monthly fee is a good investment for them plus you get regular income. You'll write 2-4 blogs a month, maybe more.

Some companies will ask you to 'repurpose' content which means you take existing blogs and articles and rewrite this content—so it looks fresh. It's fine, provided the content comes from the company that's hiring you. You have to be careful about copyright when you write a blog based on other blogs.

You should not write a blog/article for less than $50 per blog/article.

A typical blog is around 500 words, though some companies may want high-quality blogs of 1,500-2,000 words to improve their search rankings.

If the client is too demanding about grammar, style, and other items, charge them more or fire them. There is no need to get hyper-anal about grammar and style in blogs and articles.

Some clients will want you to operate in the 'back end' of a blogging site like Wordpress. So you'll need to know how to use the Wordpress dashboard. Again—that's where *your* blog is important. You'll need to know how to include photos and widgets. Here's a great example of a site with superb photos and social media widgets. (www.stuckintherockies.com).

You must be able to write quickly and clearly. I can write a 500 word blog in 30 minutes. You cannot afford to take a day to write a 500 word blog.

Summary

There's a reason I put this chapter first in the book: there's an ocean of blogging and article work out there...and you're a thimble. If you're starting from square one, blogging and article work, while sometimes tedious, provides a quick way to earn regular income while you develop other business that's more enjoyable and/or more lucrative.

Check out this page on my site (https://www.scottmartincopywriter. com/free-downloads) for additional resources and to receive regular updates about opportunities for professional writers.

Writing Press Releases and Public Relations

ublic Relations (also known as PR) is a broad field. It's also a field that requires a significant amount of writing. A PR firm or a PR specialist will handle the following:

- Press releases
- Speeches
- Press materials
- Social media
- Writing and managing blogs
- Reputation management
- Disaster planning
- Liaising with the media
- Website content
- Annual reports
- And more...

The primary role of a public relations firm is to help a company communicate its message to the public, either directly, or through media outlets. For example, a PR specialist may contact a reporter at a newspaper to encourage the reporter to write an article about a company or person. If there's a story about a company, the media will contact the company's "spokesperson" who is often a PR professional.

Yes, a PR specialist or PR firm will build relationships with media outlets and journalists, but a chunk of their time is spent writing. I describe some of the writing disciplines in more detail in later chapters but a PR writer must be flexible. One day they're writing a speech, the next they're writing a PR plan. However, for a writer, PR provides significant opportunities.

How to Break Into PR

You'll find a slew of PR companies in major cities, and you'll even find them in smaller markets. Many will hire remotely, but most will require their writers to live in their market. When contacting a PR firm for work, it helps to have a wide variety of samples in your portfolio. Larger companies usually have in-house PR people. PR is also called "public affairs."

What You Can Expect to Earn

While PR companies have become more important in the Internet age, and thus more in demand, the pay for associates in a PR firm is usually fairly modest. Depending on location, salaries for PR specialists range from $35K to $80K. However, you can always freelance for PR firms; remember, they need a lot of writing and content.

Street Smart Advice

From my experience, PR people are generally pleasant and professional. When looking for work in this field, look for firms with contracts with major companies. These firms will have the most money to spend on writing...and will have the most work.

Additional Information

The world is full of PR organizations. And most of them have job boards. Go through some of these sites to gain additional insight into the day-to-day work of a PR specialist.

Council of Public Relation Firms: http://prfirms.org/

Public Relations Society of America: http://www.prsa.org/

Public Relations Society of America – JOB CENTER: http://www.prsa.org/Jobcenter/

Public Relations Organization International: http://www.proi.com/Public/

Canadian Public Relations Society: www.cprs.ca

The Conference Board: www.conference-board.org

Corporate Watch: www.corpwatch.org

Council of PR Firms: http://prfirms.org

European Association of Communication Directors: www.eacd-online.eu

International Public Relations Association: www.ipra.org

Public Relations Consultants Association UK: www.prca.org.uk

UK Charted Institute of Public Relations: www.cipr.co.uk

International Communication Consultancy Organization (ICCO): www.iccopr.com

Council of Public Relation Firms – CAREER CENTER: http://career-center.prfirms.org/

Council of Public Relation Firms: http://prfirms.org/

International Public Relations Association: http://www.ipra.org/

Public Relations Consultants Association of the UK – JOB BOARDS: http://www.prca.org.uk/pr-jobs

Canadian Public Relations Society: http://www.cprs.ca/

Canadian Public Relations Society – JOB BOARD: http://www.cprs.ca/careers/

CPRS Career File

The National Black Public Relations Society: http://www.nbprs.org/

Summary

Public Relations is an important function for companies of all sizes, especially larger companies. While personal contact is important, at least 75% of PR work is writing. Increasingly, PR is expanding to incorporate all the new media...like blogging, social media, etc.

Corporate Communications

orporate communication is closely related to public relations. In fact, in many organizations, the PR group is part of the corporate communications division. Plus, there are firms and agencies that specialize in corporate communication. And like PR, corporate communication requires a lot of writing. If you're someone who enjoys the corporate environment and the (relative) security of a big company, then you might enjoy this niche.

People in this side of the business often handle the following:

- Corporate branding and communicating the benefits of the brand
- Corporate identity and positioning
- Corporate responsibility and philanthropy
- Building the company's reputation
- General communication with associates and customers
- Crisis management and communication
- Investor relations
- Speeches and events
- Managing websites and producing content

For example, someone in the corporate communications department might have the responsibility of sending timely information to shareholders. They might also be in charge of the company's annual report. Another associate might be the person who writes the speeches that executives deliver at conferences. Someone else might be in charge of the company's newsletters. Again...it's a broad field with plenty of room for writers. You can work in a company's department or work for a communications company; there can be opportunities for freelancers.

The writing is straightforward and even somewhat vanilla. It's corporate!

How to Break Into Corporate Communications

Many entry-level jobs are internships although companies regularly hire new graduates to enter the field. It can help to have a degree in a related discipline. Writers should scan company websites for jobs in corporate communications. Freelancers can directly contact the head of corporate communications.

What You Can Expect to Earn

Because these jobs are with major companies, they often pay pretty well. And writing for the corporate environment can provide lucrative work for freelancers. You can expect to earn $70K to $100K at the associate level once you have established yourself, but this can take several years of work. If you climb the corporate ladder and get to VP or EVP level, you can earn upwards of $150K. However, as you move up in the department, you will write less and manage more.

Street Smart Advice

For writers, the corporate communication environment can be a good place to work. Many freelancers specialize in this arena and earn a healthy living. The writing will not be terribly exciting but there will plenty of opportunity to write.

Additional Information

The primary organization for the industry is the International Association of Business Communicators: www.iabc.com/.

You might also try the Communications Media Management Association (https://cmma.org) or the International Communications Association (https://www.icahdq.org/default.aspx).

Summary

Very quietly, corporate communication provides a wealth of writing work for the writer who enjoys a variety of work in a corporate environment. The actual writing, however, can be bland and dull.

News Reporter/Journalist

D espite the arrival of new media, there are plenty of opportunities to write as a news reporter, also known as a journalist. Newspapers, news-based radio stations, and television stations still exist and remain viable businesses. And news-based websites need journalists.

Journalists report on news...either local, regional, national, or international. You'll find journalists in radio stations, TV stations, newspapers, and national news organizations like National Public Radio, the BBC, and CBS. Journalists can cover anything from business deals to deaths from wars to hurricanes.

As a journalist, you'll be asked to develop reliable sources, get the raw information, and create news stories that provide the public with valuable information.

Let's say you work for a radio station. One evening, there's an emergency at the airport where an airplane's landing gear isn't working. You'll be required to rush to the airport, liaise with the public relations officer, then follow events and record a report. Let's say you work for a newspaper and a local high school has just appointed a new principal. You'll have to read the press release, get reaction from parents and teachers, and write a story. Let's say you work for a TV station and there's been a bad car accident that's closed a major road. You'll have to rush to the scene and start reporting...live on TV.

Journalists come in all shapes and sizes. The person who covers sports for a small local newspaper is a journalist. The people on 60 Minutes are journalists. The person who reports for a news website is a journalist.

The Internet revolution has pounded journalists. Newspapers have slashed the number of journalists, and so job opportunities are poor. It's a very difficult environment. And it doesn't help that universities keep pumping out young journalists.

How to Break Into Journalism

Most journalists break into the trade by getting an internship and/or going to journalism school at a university. TV stations, radio stations, and newspapers rarely advertise for open positions...they're too busy laying people off!

What You Can Expect to Earn

Entry-level journalists can make close to $25,000 a year which is close to the poverty line...especially in a big city! However, become a star on 60 Minutes and you'll make a lot more...well into 7-figures. Highly specialized journalists and reporters who cover specific industries can earn more...close to 6 figures in some instances.

Even during the golden era of newspapers when they had a virtual monopoly on the news and were earning profit margins well over 25%, there were plenty of people who wanted to become journalists. So pay has always been extraordinarily poor. Freelancers are treated like dirt, for the most part, and I remember a local newspaper once offering me $10 to cover a basketball game. If you want to become a journalists, it has to be a vocation.

Street-Smart Advice

If you want to save the world and believe that you can generally affect the way the world operates, then you might like to become a journalist. But it's always going to be difficult to earn a significant income.

Additional Information

In the United States, the main publication is Editor and Publisher (http://www.editorandpublisher.com). You might also visit the Online News Association (http://journalists.org). Other organizations include the Society of Professional Journalists (https://www.spj.org/index.asp) and the Pew Center, which provides a list of organizations (https://www.journalism.org/).

Summary

Journalism, especially investigative journalism, plays a vital role in society. However, it's difficult to get too excited about opportunities in the field. The old model is dead and the fragmentation in the business means there are plenty of opportunities but for little pay. However, many journalists absolutely love their work...so go figure. The writing is straightforward to the point of being boring, and you'll have your work beaten up almost daily by hyper-anal copy editors. Lovely!

For additional resources and to receive regular updates about opportunities for professional writers, go here (https://www.scottmartincopywriter.com/-for-copywriters-only).

Writing for the Web

In the last chapter, I wrote about the decline of journalism. The reason: the Web, a.k.a the Internet. While it's been terrible for journalists, the Web has provided massive opportunities for writers. So this chapter is a little different...the goal of this chapter is to introduce you to all the opportunities available on the Web.

- There are 14 billion web pages and most need copy. If each web page has an average of 200 words, that's...well...a lot of writing!

- The search engines LOVE fresh content...in other words, fresh writing. So the content must be refreshed.

- Each site that sells something must rely on words to sell. Yes, images are important but it's the words that really sell.

- Many sites provide information. This means they must have information to provide. This means they must have plenty of writing.

- Many websites have blogs and sites like Wordpress have thousands of new blogs every day. Blogs typically have 300-1,000 words of copy.

- Just about everything that's printed ends up on the Web.

- Books are increasingly available on the Web either directly on Web pages or on eBooks.

If you're thinking about becoming a professional writer and you're not sure about where to start, this guide will help you. But also spend a day cruising around the web going to all sorts of different places and you'll discover the infinite variety of writing on the Web. While you're cruising around, get a sense of what interests you and this will provide some initial direction.

The American Writers and Artists Institute (AWAI) provides numerous resources for writers who want to write for the web. Discover more at awai.com.

OPPORTUNITY #6

Newspaper, Website, or Magazine Columnist

While most newspaper and magazine columnists are trained as journalists, newspaper and magazine columnists are not journalists, as such. You'll see their work next to the articles, but it's not journalism. Columnists are paid to provide opinion. I also include the people who write editorials in newspapers.

In most newspapers, columnists write 3-4 times a week. Many specialize in a field, like sports, while others will write about pretty much everything. In a magazine or on a website, a columnist might specialize in writing about being a mother...or father. From a writing standpoint, newspaper and magazine columnists get a bit more width to be creative. In fact, columnists often develop their own style. For example, there's a columnist in my local newspaper who is also a poet. She likes really short sentences. Really.

But the work is actually incredibly easy. You don't have to worry about gathering facts...you simply add color and controversy to the magazine, website, or newspaper.

How to Break In

Most newspaper and magazine columnists started as journalists then asked to become columnists. In some business-related publications, columnists are business people who write for additional income or to promote themselves.

What You Can Expect to Earn

In many newspapers and magazines and on many websites, the columnists are the rock stars. That's because they provide, as I wrote earlier, the color and controversy. When columnists leave, or get fired, readers often howl in displeasure. So many columnists earn more than regular journalists...but that's not saying much! One advantage: in a bigger market, you can become relatively famous.

Street-Smart Advice

To become a columnist, you're going to spend some time as a journalist. But you must be willing to be controversial and irritate people. You must be the person at the bar who makes things up, generally worries very little about the facts, and be loud and opinionated.

Additional Information

Associations and groups: as for journalism. However, there's a national association for columnists: The National Society of Newspaper Columnists (https://www.columnists.com). The main publication is Editor and Publisher (http://www.editorandpublisher.com). You might also visit the Online News Association (http://journalists.org). Other organizations include the Society of Professional Journalists (https://www.spj.org/index.asp) and the Pew Center, which provides a list of organizations (https://www.journalism.org/).

Summary

Just about every journalist wants to be a columnist. Why? The pay can be higher plus there's less work. You may get to travel a little. You also get more opportunity to be more creative...and controversial.

Features Writer

Features writers are more common in magazines and on websites. The bigger newspapers often run long features. A feature story is essentially a long piece of journalism. For example, a long magazine article about a movie star is a feature article. Again, a background in journalism is vital, but writing features is extremely different from day-to-day journalism. Many investigative journalists are really writing features.

For freelance writers who target magazines, writing feature stories can be lucrative. But there's a lot of work involved. A feature story requires significant research and will require at least 2,000 words. Plus, the editor will likely require numerous tweaks and changes.

How You Can Break In

To start writing features for newspapers, magazines, and websites, you'll need to be a reporter first. If you go through journalism school, you can build some pieces in your portfolio. If you're a freelancer, the idea you pitch to an editor can be more important than tons of experience.

What You Can Expect to Earn

At magazines and websites, outstanding features writers can earn more than "rank and file" journalists. Certain magazines will pay a good fee for a freelance feature story...$5,000 or more.

Street-Smart Advice

If you work full-time for a news organization, writing features can be a great gig. The day-to-day pressure is off because you have more time to research and write. Sometimes, editors assign stories but editors always need great ideas, so you can be creative and write about what you find you interesting.

Additional Information

There's the Society for Features Journalism (https://featuresjournalism. org), but you'll want to start with the organizations that help journalists. The main publication is Editor and Publisher (http://www.editorandpublisher. com) You might also visit the Online News Association (http://journalists.org). Other organizations include the Society of Professional Journalists (https://www.spj.org/index.asp) and the Pew Center, which provides a list of organizations (https://www.journalism.org/). You can start with the American Society of Journalists and Authors (https://asja.org).

Music Writer

I f you love music, any type of music, and you can write, then you can write about music...and earn money by writing about your passion. Music is such a massive and important part of daily life. It's an industry. In later chapters, I write about songwriting and writing lyrics, but there are hundreds of writers who simply write about the music.

Go to a symphony concert, and you'll buy a program. Someone has to write and publish the program. An orchestra must have a website, a newsletter, fundraising letters, and more...the orchestra must communicate frequently with its public. And, of course, orchestras increasingly rely on social media to communicate; this requires writing and social media expertise.

Let's switch to jazz. Even in a relatively small country like Scotland (population 5 million) there are numerous jazz festivals throughout the year. A jazz festival requires A TON of writing. Website. Emails. Social media. Bios. Press releases. And more.

There are hundreds of publications devoted just to music. The Strad (https://www.thestrad.com) is a magazine, and a great one, about stringed instruments. For double bass players, there's the International Society of Bassists (https://www.isbworldoffice.com/default.asp), and they have a magazine, website, etc. They need a lot of copy...and that's just in the double bass world.

Just about every newspaper in the world has a music writer and the bigger ones have very specific music writers...one to cover classical...one to cover pop/ rock...one to cover jazz, even. Smaller newspapers rely on syndicated content.

Because musicians are so devoted to music and are so passionate about their passion, they will devour information. So there's a huge need for content about music. Many musicians supplement their income by writing about music. Go to Amazon or your local bookstore, and you'll find big sections devoted to music...how to play...theory...the business of music... reviews...biographies...and more. Music writing is quietly a huge field.

How You Can Break In

What type of music do you enjoy the most? Are you a jazz freak? Is rap your bag? Music writing is an area where you'll want to specialize and become an authority. People who publish music writing are often looking for writers, so contact the publications directly. If you want to break into this field, you can start a blog and build a social media platform around your blog. You can also contact record companies, promoters, bands, musical societies, and orchestras. But the best way to start is to create your own content. Having an ebook in music would also help.

What You Can Expect to Earn

The good news...there's plenty of demand for music writing. And there always will be. The bad news...the people with the need for music writing rarely have big budgets. You're going to spend a lot of time researching and writing, but you're not to get truly fair compensation. You might break through with a book that becomes a bestseller but it's always going to be tough to make a big income writing for the music world. While part of the music world is for-profit, a chunk of the music world is non-profit with extremely limited budgets and constant cash-flow issues.

Street-Smart Advice

I'm not certain that writing full-time about music is a great way to earn steady income. You must be super-dedicated or have a marketing job with a large music organization. Writing about music can be an excellent way to supplement your income...especially if you're a musician.

Social media and publicity are especially important for musicians today. If I were entering this field as a writer, I'd position myself as providing these services, which, as we all know, require a ton of music writing and knowledge.

Grant Writer

Non-profit organizations heavily rely on grant money to meet annual budget goals. In fact, grant money can be the lifeblood of many non-profits.

Here's how it works.

A non-profit needs money. The government or a foundation has the money to give in the form of grant money. To get that money, the non-profit must write a grant proposal. And that's where the grant writer comes in; the non-profit relies on the grant writer to write the grant proposal that will persuade the government agency or foundation to write a check.

Thus grant writing is really sales writing. There's a significant demand for highly-skilled grant writers who can help non-profits mine money from the government and foundations.

A non-profit organization will ask the grant writer to research what the government or the foundation requires, then create a professional and thorough proposal. In many cases, the proposal can follow a generally accepted template.

How You Can Break In

Grant writing provides a significant opportunity for freelance and full-time writers. If you have writing skills, you can start by volunteering to help a non-profit organization with a grant proposal. Non-profits are always looking for volunteers. Once you've had some success writing grant proposals, then you can contact non-profits and say, "I've had success helping non-profits get money from the government and from foundations." This statement will resonate with non-profits.

What You Can Expect to Earn

The bigger non-profit organizations will likely have an in-house grant writer or maybe even a team of grant writers under their fundraising umbrella. A complete rookie can expect to earn around $35,000 at the high end. A super-experienced grant writer can expect to earn upwards of $100,000 but will have other fundraising responsibilities.

As a freelancer, you can earn a fee for writing proposals. Some organizations might give you a percentage of the amount funded. Remember...non-profits are often run just like a regular business so there's often an incentive for exceptional performance.

Street-Smart Advice

Because the regular staff at a non-profit organization are usually highly overworked, there's plenty of demand for grant writers with a strong record of success. You can really benefit by being professional and providing adjunctive services so that you're more than just a grant writer. You have a more powerful platform when you can provide additional "done for you" services like research and follow-up. You're always going to get the attention of a non-profit organization when you say, "I'm here to help you get money from the government and foundations." That's more compelling than, "I'm a grant writer."

How to Get Started

Because grant writing is such an important part of the non-profit arena, there are numerous resources available for grant-writers.

Here you go...

The Grant Professionals Association (GPA) hails itself as the top organization for grant writers (https://www.grantprofessionals.org). Members of the GPA include:

- Grant proposal developers
- Grant administrators and program managers
- Directors of development
- Program development directors and specialists
- Grantmakers and funders
- Proposal and program evaluators
- Independent consultants
- Grantsmanship trainers and other service providers
- Executive directors and board members of public and private organizations

They also have a job center.

The Minnesota Council on Foundations offers a guide to writing a successful proposal. (www.mcf.org/nonprofits/successful-grant-proposal).

Grant Space offers several online courses to help grant writers. (https://grantspace.org/topics/fundraising/).

You should also check out:

The Association of Fund Raising Professionals (https://afpglobal.org) and the American Grant Writers Association (http://www.agwa.us); the latter has a jobs page.

If you're interested in specializing in the environmental niche, check out the Environmental Grant Writers Association (https://ega.org).

And finally, you can find grant writing jobs on all the major job sites like Career Builder, Monster, and Simply Hired.

Noted copywriter Bob Bly provides numerous resources for writers ... including information about this niche - bly.com.

Writing for Non-Profits

I n the previous chapter, I detailed just ONE of the opportunities available for writers in the non-profit environment. Non-profits, which, perhaps, I should call not-for-profits, need to communicate internally and externally. In the smaller non-profits, staff will handle the writing work. However, in the larger organizations, you'll find numerous writers. For example, The Arthritis Foundation publishes their own magazine. Non-profits need to publish newsletters, fundraising letters, emails, and maintain a social media presence.

How You Can Break In

Show up and say, "I'm here to write for free." Smaller non-profits will happily give you plenty of work so you can build a portfolio. Then you can start to submit samples to the larger non-profits.

What You Can Expect to Earn

At the smaller non-profits, if you're on the staff, you're going to write a lot. Salaries at smaller non-profits are often extremely low. However, at the larger non-profits like The United Way, The Red Cross, etc., you can earn a competitive salary as a full-time writer...around $45,000 at the mid-range. The larger organizations often hire freelancers at competitive rates; these larger organizations are run more like for-profit businesses and pay accordingly. In most cases, the key to earning a significant income is becoming the "Director of Communications" who is really a writer in disguise!

Street-Smart Advice

Non-profits need significant quantities of writing but have limited budgets. So writing for non-profits requires some degree of vocational and philanthropic drive. If it's a serious career move, you'll need to write for the larger non-profits, and it can really help if your arsenal includes the ability to raise funds.

Writing Children's Books

Writing books for young children can be an extremely lucrative, and enjoyable, niche. Numerous children's writers have become mega-starts and earned millions in royalties. Perhaps you've heard of J.K. Rowling.

Ian Fleming, who wrote the James Bond novels, also wrote books for children. Parents want their children to read, and local and state governments have big budgets to buy books.

You can become highly specialized in this arena. For example, you can write for toddlers or teens...and every niche in between.

Even better, the digital revolution has made it even easier to get published and earn fast income from children's books. Several authors are doing very well publishing books for children on Amazon's Kindle platform. However, other authors choose to go through the somewhat arduous and slow process of going through the "traditional" book publishing process.

Before writing a word, or hiring an editor or illustrator, I recommend that everyone who wants to become a children's author thoroughly learn precisely how the business works. There's plenty of room for authors in this arena but even one false step and you'll be spinning your wheels very quickly.

How You Can Break In

In today's book publishing environment, I would not recommend going the route of traditional publishing. I would start by using Amazon's Kindle platform. Several information marketers have published guides to making the most of this platform. Once you have a sense of how digital publishing works, you can decide whether you want to move forward. You can also self-publish a physical book.

Next, take these steps...

- Choose your niche in the children's market.
- Look closely at the other books in your niche.
- Find at least two books about writing for children.
- Write your book.
- Hire a professional editor to edit the book.
- Get the book published initially on Amazon's Kindle platform and learn how to promote the book.
- Use social media to promote the book.

Once you have some experience with a first book, you can decide if you want to self-publish a physical book. If you enjoy significant online sales, you have something you can sell to a real, live publisher.

A quick Google search for "How to Become a Children's Author" will instantly provide at least two days of reading.

Here are the generally accepted niches, also known as genres.

- Picture books
- General fiction for children
- Teenage Fiction (Young Adult)
- Non-fiction

What You Can Expect to Earn

Many authors have enjoyed massive hits with children's books. They get these books turned into movies and get merchandising rights, etc. Getting to that level of multi-million dollar success is achievable, but you'll need a strong idea plus some luck. If you want to get into this arena to earn massive cash, then take a long look at who has been super-successful and how they earned their millions. But the chances of succeeding are extremely slim. Give it a shot but don't give up your day job.

If writing a book is more of a hobby, then you can earn some income from selling physical books and perhaps from your Kindle account on Amazon. However, some authors have earned several hundred thousand from the Kindle platform.

This market is massive...a multi-billion dollar annual market. Parents and schools are looking for books. Publishers must have content. Plus they must have fresh content...and that means they must have authors.

Street-Smart Advice

You have two options when it comes to writing books.

- A hobby
- A serious business venture

You can treat the writing as a hobby and use the self-publishing route to get some books in the marketplace. You can have a party at home and sell these books. There's nothing wrong with this route, provided you understand that it's a hobby...like building model cars or collecting bowling balls.

If you want to treat being a children's author as a serious business venture then you must:

- Choose a niche
- Hone your writing skills
- See what's worked for super-successful writers

- Read everything you can about publishing
- Understand precisely how the various publishing platforms work
- Be extremely patient and persistent. Every big-time children's author faced years of rejection.

Either take this extremely seriously or treat it as a hobby. Get stuck in the middle, and you'll quickly waste a lot of time and money.

For additional resources and to receive regular updates about opportunities for professional writers, go here (https://www.scottmartincopy-writer.com/-for-copywriters-only).

Songwriter

If you listen to the radio, or visit the supermarket, you hear songs. You might listen to current hits. Or you might listen to oldies. Or a jazz station. Songwriters write the songs. In the next chapter, I specifically discuss writing just the lyrics for songs. In this chapter, I focus more on the musical side. You've heard of some of the more famous songwriters...like Lennon/McCartney.

Songwriters start with a blank sheet of paper, just like all writers, then have to create a song. There's a creative side, but also a business side. If you're musical but also have a poet in you, you can try to write songs.

Some rock bands and artistes write their own songs. Some "cover" the songs that others have written. Many performers are constantly looking for fresh songs they can record. Frank Sinatra didn't write his own songs; he relied on some of the world's top songwriters.

There's a parallel with writing children's books. Treat it as a hobby or treat it as a serious business.

However, here's a basic process for getting songs published.

You'll need to write the song, including writing the song on sheet music.

Produce a recording of the song called a demo package.

Pitch the song through a marketplace. Or you can go directly to music publishers. There are several online marketplaces.

Publishers are in touch with the artists and will pitch the song.

Understand how the modern copyright process works.

Make sure you're registered with one of the big music royalty companies like BMI.

If an artists performs your song, or it appears on an album or even in a supermarket, then you're likely entitled to a royalty.

Here's a site with helpful links (www.pearlsnapstudios.com/helpful-links.html). You can also visit one of the big music companies, BMI (www.bmi.com).

How You Can Break In

The barriers to entry are essentially non-existent, especially with today's technology. If you're even half-way musical and you can write some lyrics, you've got a song. You'll need to understand the basic structure of a song then follow the basic instructions above.

You don't have to be an established writer to write a hit song. You just have to have the song and understand the publishing process.

What You Can Expect to Earn

The songwriting business works a lot like most of the other writing niches: 10% of the songwriters earn about 90% of the income from selling the song rights and from royalties. However, once you get a song published and recorded, you get a royalty each time it's performed. So you get residual income...income while you sleep. The songwriting business is highly speculative and you'll write a lot of songs that produce no income.

Street-Smart Advice

If you want to be a commercially-successful songwriter, then it's VITAL to understand how the business of songwriting works. This will ensure you'll get paid for the work. Thoroughly research all the links below.

Nashville Songwriters Association International (AKA National Songwriters Association). http://www.nashvillesongwriters.com/

Songwriters Guild of America (http://www.songwritersguild.com).

American Society of Composers, Authors, and Publishers (http://www.ascap.com)

Top Job Boards

***Songwriters Guild of America – Professional Services (https://www.songwritersguild.com/site/professional-services)

*

Nashville Songwriters Association International (AKA National Songwriters Association) http://www.nashvillesongwriters.com/

The Nashville Songwriters Association International (NSAI) consists of a body of creative minds, including songwriters from all genres of music, professional and amateur, who are committed to protecting the rights and future of the profession of songwriting, and to educate, elevate, and celebrate the songwriter and to act as a unifying force within the music community and the community at large.

***Songwriters Guild of America (http://www.songwritersguild.com)

The Songwriters Guild of America is comprised of three entities:

The Songwriters Guild of America (SGA), itself, which offers education, advocacy, services and events to advance the goals of its professional and developing songwriters.

The Songwriters Guild of America Foundation, a non-profit agency that offers services to communities and populations, especially those underserved in the arts, and music, in particular.

The Songwriters Guild of America Professional Services, including Catalog Administration, Royalty Collection, Copyright Administration and a host of other services designed to ensure that professional songwriters' earnings are protected.

Songwriters Guild of America – Professional Services (http://www.songwritersguild.com)

American Society of Composers, Authors, and Publishers (http://www.ascap.com)

ASCAP, an organization owned and run by its members, is the leading U.S. Performing Rights Organization representing over 450,000 songwriters, composers and music publishers.

National Music Publisher's Association (http://nmpa.org)

The National Music Publishers' Association is the largest U.S. music publishing trade association with over 3,000 members. Its mission is to protect, promote, and advance the interests of music's creators. The NMPA is the voice of both small and large music publishers, the leading advocate for publishers and their songwriter partners in the nation's capital and in every area where publishers do business. The goal of NMPA is to protect its members' property rights on the legislative, litigation, and regulatory fronts. In this vein, the NMPA continues to represent its members in negotiations to shape the future of the music industry by fostering a business environment that furthers both creative and financial success. The NMPA has remained the most active and vocal proponent for the interests of music publishers in the U.S. and throughout the world, a continuing tradition of which the association is very proud.

Broadcast Music Inc (http://www.bmi.com/about/)

Broadcast Music, Inc. (BMI) collects license fees on behalf of the more than 550,000 songwriters, composers, and music publishers it represents and distributes those fees as royalties to members whose works have been publicly performed.

Lyricist

If you barely have a musical bone in your body, but you're a writer and you think you can write the words for songs, then you could be a lyricist or, in operatic terminology, a librettist.

For example, you may have heard of the musical, Evita. Andrew Lloyd-Weber wrote the music and Tim Rice wrote the words. Tim Rice was the lyricist.

In chapter 12, I wrote about writing songs. Lyricists write the words for songs but also write words for operas, musicals, and additional music.

Many songwriters can write a good tune and some good music. But most are poor when it comes to the words. So writers can earn income by writing the words to the songs and other music. You'll want to team up with a musician who wants to write musicals, songs, etc.

How You Can Break In

As with songwriting, the barriers to entry are almost non-existent. You can write the lyrics for a song and perform the song instantly. You can get the song published and others can perform the song...and that's where you generate the income.

What You Can Expect to Earn

For songs, you earn a royalty each time the song is performed, and you have to register with one of the royalty distribution companies (see above). With a musical or opera, or similar type of music, you get paid almost immediately after the performance...thus much, much faster. You get paid a percentage of the gate for each performance. Very quietly, people like Tim Rice have earned fortunes writing lyrics.

Street-Smart Advice

Bob Dylan writes complex song lyrics. But most song lyrics are almost mindlessly simple. The key is having a sense of what sounds right...and complements the music. Hook up with a musician, listen to the great songs, and fully understand how the music business works. At the very least, you'll go to a dive bar to hear a garage band perform your lyrics. Get with the right musician and you could potentially earn a significant income.

Note: to understand the business side, here are the links from chapter 12.

Nashville Songwriters Association International (AKA National Songwriters Association). http://www.nashvillesongwriters.com/

Songwriters Guild of America (http://www.songwritersguild.com)

American Society of Composers, Authors, and Publishers http://www.ascap.com/

Top Job Boards

***Songwriters Guild of America – Professional Services http://www.sga-cap.com/services.html

*

Nashville Songwriters Association International (AKA National Songwriters Association) http://www.nashvillesongwriters.com/

The Nashville Songwriters Association International (NSAI) consists of a body of creative minds, including songwriters from all genres of music, professional and amateur, who are committed to protecting the rights and future of the profession of songwriting, and to educate, elevate, and celebrate the songwriter and to act as a unifying force within the music community and the community at large.

***Songwriters Guild of America http://www.songwritersguild.com/sandboxsga2010/index.html

The Songwriters Guild of America is comprised of three entities:

The Songwriters Guild of America (SGA), itself, which offers education, advocacy, services and events to advance the goals of its professional and developing songwriters.

The Songwriters Guild of America Foundation, a non-profit agency that offers services to communities and populations, especially those underserved in the arts, and music, in particular.

The Songwriters Guild of America Professional Services, including Catalog Administration, Royalty Collection, Copyright Administration and a host of other services designed to ensure that professional songwriters' earnings are protected.

Songwriters Guild of America – Professional Services http://www.sga-cap.com/services.html

American Society of Composers, Authors, and Publishers http://www.ascap.com/

ASCAP, an organization owned and run by its members, is the leading U.S. Performing Rights Organization representing over 450,000 songwriters, composers and music publishers.

National Music Publisher's Association http://www.nmpa.org/home/index.asp

The National Music Publishers' Association is the largest U.S. music publishing trade association with over 3,000 members. Its mission is to protect, promote, and advance the interests of music's creators. The NMPA is the voice of both small and large music publishers, the leading advocate for publishers and their songwriter partners in the nation's capital and in every area where publishers do business. The goal of NMPA is to protect its members' property rights on the legislative, litigation, and regulatory fronts. In this vein, the NMPA continues to represent its members in negotiations to shape the future of the music industry by fostering a business environment that furthers both creative and financial success. The NMPA has remained the most active and vocal proponent for the interests of music publishers in the U.S. and throughout the world, a continuing tradition of which the association is very proud.

Broadcast Music Inc http://www.bmi.com/about/

Broadcast Music, Inc. (BMI) collects license fees on behalf of the more than 550,000 songwriters, composers, and music publishers it represents and distributes those fees as royalties to members whose works have been publicly performed.

Ghostwriting

Millions of people want to get published, but only a small percentage have the time and the talent. Thus there's a big market for ghostwriters.

- The time
- The talent

The ghostwriter is the writer who actually writes the book...when it may be attributed to another person.

For example, golfer Arnold Palmer didn't write his autobiography. He hired, or the publisher hired, James Dodson to write the book. If you look at the current New York Times bestsellers list, you'll see a lot of famous authors. Only a few of them actually wrote the book...especially in the non-fiction side.

But ghostwriters write much more than books. They write blogs, articles, speeches, and much more. Hook up with a professional or celebrity and they can provide a steady stream of consistent ghostwriting work.

It's fairly easy to ghostwrite a blog or article. Ghostwriting a book is significantly more complex. That's due to the sheer scale of the project.

How to Break In

On the major sites that list work for writers, like elance.com and freelance switch, you'll find plenty of professionals who need ghostwriting help for articles, blogs, and related needs. You can also contact business people you know and pitch them on the idea of writing articles and blogs for them.

When it comes to big-time book publishing, you'll need to have experience writing for, or working in, a major publishing house...probably in New York City. You can also try contacting the publishing houses directly with a portfolio of articles and blogs that you've ghostwritten.

What You Can Expect to Earn

You can charge anywhere from $50 to $250 for a ghostwritten blog, more for an article. Ghostwriters usually a receive a fee for ghostwriting books and this can vary from $5,000 to $100,000 depending on the project. You can also receive a portion of the royalties, depending on the deal. You'll need to work with a literary agent.

Street-Smart Advice

For regularly weekly work that pays decently, it can be valuable to develop ghostwriting work for executives. It can be tough to break into the New York Literary Scene when it comes to ghostwriting but working on books can be rewarding. Many executives want to publish a book privately to enhance their careers and this can lead to some big projects. It helps if you can also provide additional publishing services.

For additional information, you can try the Association of Ghostwriters (https://associationofghostwriters.org).

For additional resources and to receive regular updates about opportunities for professional writers, go here (https://www.scottmartincopywriter.com/-for-copywriters-only).

Essay Writing

Before the digital revolution, magazines and publications targeted at amateur or professional intellectuals were the main place to publish essays. These publications still exist, which is important, but today, the main platform for the essay is the blog. And several websites/blogs have popped up which are dedicated to publishing serious, or not-so-serious essays.

There's a lot to be said for the essay. It's an expression of thought and a vital part of maintaining free speech in today's society. You'll also find essays in newspapers, but they are called opinion pieces.

How to Break In

Unless you're in a position of power or you're a noted intellectual, it can be difficult to get published in a publication. But it's not impossible. If you're serious about getting published in one of these publications, contact the editor.

To get started in the blogosphere with essays, set up your own blog or contact people who run a busy blog with a bunch of traffic. These blog owners are often looking for guest blogs.

What You Can Expect to Earn

A high-brow intellectual publication will probably pay extremely poorly. Some of the top publications might pay more...up to $500 for an essay. Blogs run by companies may well pay for fresh essays relevant to their industry. Up to $250 per blog.

Street-Smart Advice

Writing blogs for other blogs can provide a useful additional source of income. If you want to be a thought-leader in your industry, then writing essays for a well-regarded publication is a good idea.

OPPORTUNITY #16

Business Plan Writing

The document that stands between an entrepreneur and project funding is a business plan. A business plan details how a new business plans to make money; some business plans detail how an established business will change. The plan will include financial details on spreadsheets but, as the writer, you only have to focus on the strategy and tactics in the plan.

Most business plans follow a standard template. Ultimately, the business plan is a sales document that tries to persuade the reader (either a banker or an investor) that the company is a safe bet.

How to Break In

You can create a "mock" business plan to show you have the skills necessary to produce a business plan. Plus, you'll find several books about writing business plans. If you have sales writing/copywriting experience, this can be helpful.

Online, you'll find plenty of bottom-fishers who are willing to overlook a relative lack of experience in return for a low price; you can build a portfolio this way. Once you're established, you can contact local bankers and let them know you write business plans; you can get referrals this way.

What You Can Expert to Earn

Once established, writing business plans can be lucrative...especially once you learn how to create them quickly. This niche is somewhat commoditized but you can write business plans for anywhere from $500 to $5,000 and more.

Street Smart Advice

You're not going to get much repeat business writing business plans...that's why it's important to develop referrals from local professionals who deal with entrepreneurs. You'll get the higher fees once you can show your plans get results. Some clients will be easy to deal with; others will be disorganized, slow, and/or poor. If you can, get your money up front in the form of a check. A real key to being successful in this business is a website showing you're the total specialist. Plus you'll need to be a complete whiz at word processing programs. Several writers have built successful businesses writing business plans.

Writing EBooks

With the arrival of the digital publishing revolution, writing ebooks has become a popular and potentially lucrative venture. It's not overly complicated. You write a book then publish the book online. There's no physical book. The book can be a PDF or you can put the book on a platform like Amazon's Kindle.

If you choose the latter, Amazon can help drive traffic to the page on Amazon's site. If you choose to publish the book yourself, you'll need to set up a web page, organize the payment through a shopping cart, then drive traffic to the page that sells your book.

Ebooks can be about just anything. One ebook details how to purify water in the event of a nuclear disaster. Another ebook is all about knitting.

How to Break In

There are virtually no barriers to entry. You simply have to write the book, understand how digital publishing works, and put your book online. Of course, it's a little more complicated but millions of people have published ebooks successfully.

However, if you really want to make a serious living writing and/or publishing ebooks, you MUST do your homework and really understand how this business works. Several companies run courses about online ebook publishing or you can find about a bazillion online courses about the subject. Like most businesses, a small portion of ebook authors make most of the money.

What You Can Expect to Earn

Ebooks range in price from around $2 to upwards of $100 for highly specialized information. Amazon's Kindle platform pays a royalty that can range from 35-70% royalty. If you self-publish, then you can keep all the revenue. However, in most cases, you're going to have to spend a chunk of cash generating traffic to your web page. Some ebook writers earn millions but most barely squeak by.

Street Smart Advice

I can't stress this enough...you MUST do your homework before getting into this fight. You can quickly spin your wheels and waste a ton of time and money. You have to understand websites, traffic, affiliate deals, and content creation. And that's just getting started.

However, there are several tools on the Internet to help established and newbie writers succeed.

As a writer, you can write your own ebooks or write them for others.

Part of the attraction of ebooks is that once you've written the book and set up the platform, you can earn money while you sleep.

Want to know more about ebook writing?

Start at Amazon's Kindle platform (https://kdp.amazon.com/self-publishing/signin).

Noted copywriter Bob Bly provides numerous resources for writers ... including information about this niche - (http://bly.com).

For additional resources and to receive regular updates about opportunities for professional writers, go here (https://www.scottmartincopywriter.com/-for-copywriters-only).

Lawyer

I've always joked that lawyers are simply writers and actors who have figured out a successful business model. Some lawyers (the actors) show up in court to fight cases, etc. The others (the writers) write contracts and other legal documents. In reality, a lawyer is really just a highly-specialized writer. Perhaps the writing isn't always that exciting...like a 100 page contract...but the work mostly pays extremely well.

How to Break In

You'll need an undergraduate degree then you'll need to go to law school. And pass the bar exam. Then you'll need to find a job with a law firm. It's not easy. But once you're in, you'll get to write a TON.

What You Can Expect to Earn

Attorneys at big law firms in big cities can expect to earn hundreds of thousands a year. Independent law firms and attorneys in smaller markets don't always make as much as people think...closer to the $60,000 range... if they're lucky.

Street Smart Advice

Becoming a lawyer isn't an automatic ticket to big money. Yes...certain lawyers can do well but the ones who write contracts and perform other writing-related tasks are increasingly becoming commoditized; the days of billing hour after hour are mostly over. The steadiest work is to be found at the larger firms. If you have even a semi-creative bone in your body, then you'll hate being a lawyer. Plus...nobody really likes attorneys, and the work is often highly contentious.

Still... if you're keen to learn more, go here: https://www.lawyeredu.org.

Paralegal

A paralegal is a legal assistant...not a lawyer but not a secretary. As such, a paralegal often has to write and prepare documents. Again, as above, the writing is not always very exciting and it's highly technical, but it's writing nonetheless.

One major benefit of being a paralegal: you don't have to go law school. Basic training is often available at a local community college or through a law firm.

How to Break In

You can start at a law firm as an assistant then move up to become a paralegal. Or you can earn the requisite qualifications then apply for jobs with law firms.

What You Can Expect to Earn

This varies greatly depending on the city and state but experienced paralegals can earn from $30K - $60K and above. Most firms will also provide benefits.

Street Smart Advice

The writing isn't creative or glamorous and it's highly technical but there's an abundance of work for reliable paralegals.

Here are some links and resources.

Top Two Associations:

***National Federation of Paralegal Association http://www.paralegals. org/ (+JOB BOARD)

***Association of Legal Assistants http://www.nala.org/

Top Job Boards

***The International Paralegal Management Association – JOB BOARD http://www.paralegalmanagement.org/management-resources/ resources-for-paralegal-managers/job-listings

*** American Bar Association – JOB BOARD http://www.american-bar.org/resources_for_lawyers/careercenter.html

National Federation of Paralegal Association – JOB BOARD http:// www.paralegals.org/default.asp?page=77

List of National and International Associations for Paralegals http:// paralegaltoday.com/links/assoc_links.htm#National

***National Federation of Paralegal Association http://www.parale-gals.org/

NFPA Headquarters
Mailing/Shipping: NFPA
23607 Highway 99, Suite 2-C
Edmonds, WA 98026
Telephone: 425-967-0045
Monday through Friday, 8:30 AM to 5:00 PM (Pacific time)
Fax: 425-771-9588
General inquiries by E-mail: info@paralegals.org

***Association of Legal Assistants http://www.nala.org/
NALA Headquarters
1516 S. Boston, #200
Tulsa, OK 74119

918-587-6828
fax: 918-582-6772

American Bar Association http://www.americanbar.org/aba.html

American Association of Paralegal Education http://www.aafpe.org/
AAFPE/American_Association_for_Paralegal_Education.asp
AAfPE Headquarters
19 Mantua Road
Mt. Royal, NJ 08061
Telephone: (856) 423-2829
Fax: (856) 423-3420
Email: info@aafpe.org
The American Alliance of Paralegals, Inc http://www.aapipara.org/

The International Paralegal Management Association http://www.
paralegalmanagement.org/

Technical Writer

L et's say you've just started a new job. On the first day, your new boss gives you a big thick manual that details how to do your job: the policies and procedures manual. Someone wrote that manual, and that someone is a technical writer. Let's say you buy a new TV and there's a manual in the box; the manual (or instruction book) is the work of a technical writer.

Technical writers write manuals, instructions, directions, and other "how to" documentation. You'll find technical writers in aerospace companies, major corporations, and in consulting firms. And also in government jobs.

The work of a technical writer rarely requires any creativity, but it's work that's necessary and vital to the functioning of many businesses and agencies. Tech companies, like Apple, employ a small army of technical writers.

How to Break In

Many colleges and universities have technical writing programs. You can also buy books to learn how to write technical literature; there are also online courses. Companies usually post jobs for technical writers on their websites and job sites. However, you may want to contact HR departments directly. You'll also find plenty of project work listed online. If you want to go the freelance route, you'll need a good website plus a LinkedIn presence.

What You Can Expect to Earn

Because technical writing is highly specialized and there's a strong demand for technical writers, you can earn a solid living working for a company or freelancing. Depending on the location, you can earn up to $40K a year to begin with salaries approaching low six figures if you're the boss in a big department. For contract work and freelancing, you can expect $30 to $60 an hour.

Street Smart Advice

If you're the creative type who wants to write fiction or if you're more interested in the marketing side of writing, then technical writing might bore you to tears. However, it can provide a useful income. If you're the engineering or technology type, you might love technical writing.

Top Two Associations:

Society for Technical Communication http://www.stc.org/

Association for Business Communication http://businesscommunication.org/

***Society for Technical Communication – JOB BOARD https://careers.stc.org/

STC provides members with a robust Job Bank and Career Center where they can search for career opportunities with leading organizations from around the world. In addition to identifying career opportunities, members can access resources designed to help technical communicators at every stage of their careers. The STC Salary Database, based on the

U.S. Department of Labor Statistics, enables members to research their compensation level as well as compare it to other metropolitan areas. Post a resume, search the job listings, or create a personal job alert to let you know when jobs you want are available. This service is free to members.

Employers and recruiters can review resumes and post jobs. Visit the Job Bank page for pricing options and more to take advantage of the experience and skills gained by hiring STC members.

German professional association for technical communication and Information-Development

***Association for Business Communication – JOB BOARD https://www.businesscommunication.org/page/job-board

The ABC Job Board provides ABC members year-round access to openings in the communication field. In the past, firms have filled positions such as technical writers, organizers of in-house publications, and public relations specialists. Academic organizations have filled teaching positions in business/organizational/managerial communication, speech communication, business education, and many other related areas. The job board complements placement services offered at the ABC Annual Convention each fall.

Institute of Scientific and Technical Communicators http://www.istc.org.uk/

SIGDOC Special Interest Group on Design of Communication http://sigdoc.acm.org/

Technical Writing Job Sites http://writingjobs.issendai.com/technical-writing-job-sites.shtml

*Just Tech Writer Jobs http://www.justtechjobs.com/

Has far more than tech writer jobs. DBA's, sysadmins, and other computer professionals can also find jobs here.

*Dice.com http://www.dice.com/

If you are a technology expert in areas such as Information Technology (IT), software, high tech, security, biotech, aerospace or engineering, Dice will assist you with finding your next great career opportunity.

*The Write Jobs: Technical Writing http://www.writejobs.com/technicalwritingjobs/

Noted copywriter Bob Bly provides numerous resources for writers ... including information about this niche. Access Bob's resources at https://www.bly.com/.

University Professor

There's an old saying in academia: Publish or Perish. Translation: you need to publish your research findings in magazines and books or you get fired. So a university professor is going to be a writer, even if they teach chemistry. Of course, if you enjoy writing, then you're going to love being a professor.

Most of the writing will back up your research. For example, if you're in the biology department, then you'll research some aspect of biology and then write a book or an article about your findings. Some professors teach writing or write about writing...in English and language departments.

How to Break In

The ultimate goal is to become a full tenured professor, AKA "Associate" professor. Or just a "Professor of..." You'll need an undergraduate degree. A masters. A doctorate. And then you'll need to apply for jobs as an assistant professor. This puts you on what's called the "tenure track." You'll teach, yes, but you'll also need to get published. At some stage, a group of your peers will decided if you can become a full professor.

What You Can Expect to Earn

This varies greatly depending on the location of the college or university. But assistant professors can earn around $40,000 while some professors make well over $100,000.

Street Smart Advice

Getting to the point where you become a full professor with tenure can be arduous. Years of school then what's essentially an apprenticeship as an assistant professor. But you will get to write a TON if you're a professor... just make sure you get published.

Direct Response Copywriter

I f you tell someone that you're a novelist, people know exactly what you do. However, if you tell someone you're a "direct response copywriter," then you'll be met with a blank stare. I know this because I'm a direct response copywriter.

Essentially, I'm more of a salesman than a writer: my words persuade people to buy products and services. You'll see my work in emails, on websites, in direct mail, and in videos. If you look in the LL Bean catalog, you'll see the work of a direct response copywriter. Ditto on an infomercial selling knives.

Direct response copywriting is difficult, and you won't find a university or college course that teaches direct response copywriting. You have to know how to write response-driven copy and you HAVE to understand how it works. The results are very closely measured. There is no place to hide.

Fortunately, there are templates that often work in direct response copywriting and you can follow one of these. It's not desperately difficult to write basic and sound direct response copy. But writing copy that really drives significant revenue is difficult and requires experience and skill.

Because direct response copywriters help companies sell products and services, there's significant demand for writers who can produce consistent, measurable results. And because there is not a steady stream of college graduates who know how to write direct response copy, there's less competition.

So...with a big demand for writers who can sell, plus a lack of writers who have the skills, direct response copywriters are among the most highly paid writers on the planet. Companies will pay high fees to a seriously good direct response copywriter, plus you can earn royalties based on sales.

Here's how it works...a company wants to sell a product or service. The company sends out a mailer or sends traffic to a website. The direct response copywriter writes the words that persuade the reader to take the next step in the sales process. This could be making a phone call, entering an email address, or asking for a direct sale.

How to Break In
You can get into direct response copywriting as a college graduate by contacting one of the big direct response companies. These companies will often hire "cub" copywriters and train them. If you're making a complete career switch, you can create some "spec" pieces then show them to prospective clients. This will help you gain valuable experience you can then show to people who need direct response copy.

Numerous books have been written about writing direct response copy. You can also find manuals and information products that tell you how to write direct response copy that produces results. Plus, I use my direct response copywriting skills to sell...well...ME!

What You Can Expect to Earn
Once you establish a solid portfolio of successful projects, you can expect to earn at least $100,000 as a freelancer. Many direct response copywriters earn significantly more because they start to earn royalties and mailing fees. A "cub" copywriter can earn at least $40,000 fairly quickly. Again...it's not easy to find copywriters who can produce, so companies have to compensate top copywriters very well.

Street Smart Advice
There are more direct response copywriters around due to several companies that provide more formal training. However, the demand for writers

who can really sell continues to increase as well. Being a direct response copywriter can be a superb gig, but you must understand that clients are going to measure the results very closely. You MUST be able to apply the techniques so you produce results. Plus you have to be able to market yourself successfully.

Additional Information

Noted copywriter Bob Bly provides numerous resources for writers ... including information about this niche - http://bit.ly/3eaJr2i.

The American Writers and Artists Institute (AWAI) provides numerous resources for writers who want to write for this niche. Discover more at their website: www.awaionline.com/go/index.php?af=1578337.

For additional resources and to receive regular updates about opportunities for professional writers, go here (https://www.scottmartincopywriter.com/-for-copywriters-only).

Email Copywriter and Email Marketing Specialist

The world continues to be full of email, which has been with us now for roughly 20 years. Email marketing, even though some people think of it as spam, is still a very important marketing tool for companies of all sizes. Small companies use it to sell their products and services and are not usually very advanced. Mid-sized companies sometimes really know what they're doing when it comes to email marketing, and other times, they're a bit clueless. Major, big companies use email a great deal, and use analytical tools and are exceptional when it comes to producing results from email marketing.

Writing emails that produce results is a skill. It requires a lot of testing. It is very close to…or should be considered…direct response copywriting. However, there are some differences between writing for a long sales page and writing emails. If you're going to be an email specialist writer, then you will also need to understand how email marketing works. You will also need to understand how the various email services work. And these services are sometimes referred to as email platforms.

Being somebody who can produce results via email is valuable and if you can present yourself as somebody who really understands email marketing and who can write successful emails, then you will be valuable to a company. You can either work inside a company or you can offer your services on a freelance basis. You can also work for advertising agencies and non-profit groups.

How to Break In

In many instances, you'll want to start a career in email writing and marketing by being with a company, preferably a large one, that really understands email marketing. However, you can also learn the techniques and learn about the current technology through online courses or by buying books, videos, and information products. You'll want to build your own database of prospective clients and email them to market yourself. There is a huge demand for people who can perform this type of service, so you don't necessarily have to have a huge amount of experience.

What You Can Expect to Earn

Entry level, you can get on with a big company in their email marketing area and probably earn at least $40,000 a year in salary. If you build a business as an email marketer, depending on who your clients are, you should be able to get three to ten clients who will pay you $500-1,000 a month. So it can be a profitable way to be a writer. And that's in part because this is all related to being a direct-response copywriter. You are helping companies produce revenue through their email databases and there's always a demand for people who can help companies create revenue.

Street Smart Advice

The companies who hire you for their email marketing efforts are going to expect to see results, so you really have to know how to write direct response copy for emails and how to measure the results and how email marketing really *really* works. You can't just show up and say, "I know how to do this." Fortunately, the major email platforms provide a ton of advice to copywriters and email marketing specialists and also provide very good service. So I think it's a solid and viable way to be a marketing writer. And if you can show people that you can produce results and help them drive revenue, there will be plenty of work for you.

Noted copywriter Bob Bly provides numerous resources for writers ... including information about this niche - http://bit.ly/3eaJr2i.

The American Writers and Artists Institute (AWAI) provides numerous resources for writers who want to write for this niche. Discover more at their website: www.awaionline.com/go/index.php?af=1578337.

For additional resources and to receive regular updates about opportunities for professional writers, go here (https://www.scottmartincopywriter.com/-for-copywriters-only).

Magazine or Newspaper Editor

Magazines and newspapers are put together by writers; the people who determine what the writers cover are the editors. And there are two different types of editor. The editor is somebody who directs the journalists and the writers. They also read through the stories; they assign the stories and they determine what happens in the newspaper or the magazine. A copy editor is somebody who takes what the writers write and edits it for clarity and punctuation and spelling. So a copy editor is not necessarily a writer, although they must know how to write.

The editor of a magazine or newspaper is usually a writer or has been a writer. Newspapers and magazines also rely on deputy editors and sub editors. So if you're somebody who loves proofreading, grammar, punctuation, and spelling, then being a copy editor is a great job for you. You'll need really outstanding attention to detail, and you'll have to understand things like style sheets. If you like management roles, and see yourself as a writer but also a supervisor or leader, then you'll enjoy being an editor at a magazine or newspaper.

How to Break In

If you go to a university or college, they will typically offer some type of copy editing course as part of getting a degree in English. You can then contact newspapers and magazines and say, "I'm a copy editor." There is also a huge amount of work online for freelance copy editors. Magazines and newspapers are usually looking for copy editors. If you want to become an editor, then you'll need to start as a journalist. You can break into journalism by going into journalism school. Sometimes newspapers and magazines hire English majors, but you'll have to have written numerous stories for other magazines or newspapers. You'll have to prove yourself as a writer and then the management will have to promote you to being an editor.

What You Can Expect to Earn

If you rise to become an editor of a big newspaper or magazine, you can expect to earn $200,000 a year to $500,000 a year, and maybe even more. As a sub-editor you are going to earn what journalists earn and the salaries are not great: $30,000 a year up to $70,000 a year. Don't forget that online publications also need editors and copy editors.

Street Smart Advice

If you really like writing and you want to stick to writing, then you probably shouldn't become a magazine editor or an editor at a newspaper. Being an editor is much more of a management and direction role. You're basically the boss, and you're telling journalists and writers what to write. Being a magazine editor or a newspaper editor also means you'll need to have political skills. However, if you enjoy the journalism environment and you just don't want to do the day-to-day work of a journalist or a writer, then being an editor can be a good choice. Rank and file journalists hate editors because editors usually make more money and do less work.

Medical Writer

There is a huge amount of demand for writers who have really strong medical backgrounds and who can also write. Medical writers can write a wide variety of copy plus you'll find the work of medical writers in medical journals. Companies that make medical products need medical writers. Advertising agencies need medical writers. Pharmaceutical companies need people with medical writing skills. Hospitals need writers; so it's a huge field where there is always a demand for writers. Some medical writers will write for regular people like you and me. Other medical writers will write for professionals in the medical field. So, if you have an interest in medicine or nutrition, or alternative health, let's say, then going into the medical field as a writer can be an excellent decision.

How to Break In

You're probably going need a degree in English from a university or college. It can also help if you have coursework in a medical field such as biology or chemistry. There are even courses in becoming a medical writer that Boston University, for example, provides. You'll probably need to go work for a pharmaceutical company or a hospital or a company that manufactures medical equipment. That can be a good place to start. And there are plenty of freelance medical writers. And of course because there's a huge demand for health care products, if you can write copy that sells health care products, there's a huge market for you. For example, there are several direct response copywriters who only write copy for nutritional supplements, and there's a big demand for writers who can handle this type of work.

What You Can Expect to Earn

Very quietly being a writer in the medical field can be a good way to earn an excellent income and even earn a really big income especially if you can help a company sell products with copywriting. You can expect to earn $40,000-50,000 working for a medical related company and you can expect to earn well over $100,000 if you're a copywriter that can help companies sell healthcare supplements and related products.

Street Smart Advice

This field is not going away, obviously, and it's only going to get bigger. If you want to be a writer who makes a good income, I would definitely strongly consider this field because you will find a spot in a hospital communications department or an advertising agency or a pharmaceutical company. However, if you can combine an interest in health and nutrition with the ability to sell products and services, there's going to be large and consistently excellent demand for your services from great companies and brands.

Branding Copywriter

I f you've ever watched television for even a few moments and you've seen the commercials, then you've seen the work of a branding copywriter. Maybe you've seen ads in a magazine, online, or in a newspaper. These ads are trying to make you feel a certain way about a certain company. And, these ads are not created to produce a specific and measurable result like a sale. Companies of all sizes want to project a good image for their brand. And, to do this, they hire advertising agencies, and within the advertising agency, there is a copywriter; the copywriter creates ads that project a good image for the brand. Being a branding copywriter can be a lot of fun because you get to be very creative. You also get to work within an advertising or marketing agency.

How to Break In

Most branding copywriters have been to university or a college to study how to become a copywriter within an agency framework. It is difficult to break into branding copywriting if you're changing careers. It's one of those things where you really need to get agency experience under your belt.

What You Can Expect to Earn

There's actually a pretty decent demand for really good branding copywriters. And while there is a pretty good supply of branding copywriters, big agencies in big cities are always looking for the best of the best. At the entry level, you can expect to earn, in a big city, maybe around $40,000- 50,000 a year. And then if you become experienced, successful, and move along, you can expect to earn well into six-figures. Especially if you use your copywriting skills and experience to move up the ladder in an advertising agency and become a creative director or even the head of an agency. Many people who run advertising agencies started as a copywriter.

Street Smart Advice

You really have to be clever, witty, and entertaining because your job is to make companies look good. And to do that, you need to create an image, and it's not an exact science. It's something that is actually very difficult to achieve. Within an advertising agency or the advertising world, there are three levels of copywriter: Junior, Mid-level, and Senior. And, after three years, you can become a mid-level copywriter. After another three to four years, you can become a senior copywriter. If you're talented and good, you can move up the ladder very quickly.

Writing Proposals

ompanies of all shapes and sizes have to write proposals in order to get business from other companies. Writing and putting together really good proposals is a highly marketable skill in the corporate environment. You can also do it as a freelancer, and smaller companies will use freelance proposal writers. Essentially what you do is follow certain proposal templates. This involves gathering facts and looking up the request for a proposal...if there is one. It also means putting together graphs, images, and doing some additional homework. Basically somebody, usually in the sales department, will come to you as the proposal writer and give you the details that you need, and then you have to write the proposal. Make sure it's polished and ready to go by the deadline. It can also help to have video skills and PowerPoint skills. However, companies put together proposals all the time and within the marketing department or the sales department, they need somebody who can put together really really great proposals.

What You Can Expect to Earn

As a freelancer, fees for proposals can range from $100 to $10,000 depending on the complexity of the proposal and the size of the proposal. Within a company, you're not going to make big cash. You're not going to earn over six-figures writing proposals but it can be a good entry-level job for a company and you'll likely get a salary between $35,000 and $70,000 a year. Not bad money, but not great either.

How to Break In

If you have a degree in English or a similar degree, you can often get an entry level job in a company in the marketing department where you can write proposals. It's the sort of position where it can be helpful to have an internship at first. So, you can you put proposals as an individual, be part of a team that puts together proposals and then you can move on to become somebody with a full-time position in a company.

Street Smart Advice

You're going to have to work under very tight deadlines sometimes. So, it's often going to mean late nights. You can sometimes have to work with difficult people who don't understand the value of what you do. However if you can show people that you can write and create proposals that produce results, there will always be a demand for your services. You also have to understand how to use all of the software tools at your disposal like Microsoft Word, PowerPoint, and so on. And you really have to be an expert at using these tools.

Noted copywriter Bob Bly provides numerous resources for writers ... including information about this niche - http://bit.ly/3eaJr2i.

Resume Writer

Many people who need a resume are very poor writers, and they don't understand how to use Microsoft Word or similar word processing programs. And thus, they go searching for people who are writing resumes. There's a big market for people who can write and produce resumes. Until a few years ago, there used to be resume writing stores, and there may still be some in larger markets; you would walk in and meet with a writer who would then produce your resume. It's all online today, or almost all online. So as a resume writer, someone will contact you, you will quote a fee, and then you will write a resume and maybe some cover letters as well. You're going to have to be an independent operator if you're going to write resumes. You're going to have to be very good at Search Engine Optimization and you'll need to create a website as well to get people to contact you.

How to Break In

You really don't need significant experience to be a resume writer. You just need to be able to produce a clean, clear resume that highlights somebody's skills. You basically need to create a website, show some samples on your website and eventually people will start contacting in order to get their resume produced and written.

What You Can Expect to Earn

You can get a super cheap resume online for about $50, but it looks like a good quality along with some cover letters can run anywhere from $200 to $500. So depending on how quickly you can produce these resumes, you can earn a pretty decent income. You're not going to get any residual income, but you can get referrals. And this can lead to additional income.

Street Smart Advice

The real key to being successful in this business is making sure that when people search for a resume writer, your website pops up. So you need to understand marketing through the web and you need to be able to sell people if they contact you. You also need to understand Search Engine Optimization and Pay Per Click advertising. You don't need to meet with potential clients. You can do it all over the telephone or Skype. You can help anyone who is needing a resume, so you can operate the small business from your home or through a small office. This can be an excellent part-time venture, however there are resume writers and cover letter writers who make this their full-time business.

Annual Report Writer

Each year, by law, every company that is publicly traded needs to produce an annual report. If you're the shareholder of a company, then you will have received an annual report. You may also have seen the digital version of it on a company's website. There are companies that specialize in producing annual reports, and some companies do them in house. There is a significant amount of writing involved in an annual report. And many companies will outsource the writing to an independent writer. The writing is not that difficult. It basically tells everybody about what happened to the company; it will include stories about people in the company and basically provide a summary of what happened during the last financial year.

How to Break In

If you want to do this as a freelancer, you'll need experience having worked in a corporate communications division or working for a company that produces annual reports.

What You Can Expect to Earn

If you work in the corporate communications division of a big company, you can expect to earn anywhere from $40,000 to $100,000 a year and your responsibilities may include writing the annual report. It can also help if you understand how to put together an annual report as well. As a freelancer, fees can vary from $5,000 to $20,000 depending on the complexity of the annual report. It's a highly specialized field and companies are typically looking for people who have a lot of experience writing annual reports.

Street Smart Advice

An annual report requires a significant amount of work. The work isn't technically that difficult but you will meet regularly with clients and a lot of people will want to see the copy before it sees the light of day. This can be an excellent opportunity for writers who like the corporate environment and enjoy writing about business.

Instructional Design

Instructional design is the creation of training materials. For example, if a company needs to train a bank teller, it has to create a PowerPoint presentation or a manual or a video...something to instruct the teller how to be a teller. Very quietly, there's a huge amount of work out there because training is such an important part of the corporate world. There are plenty of firms that specialize in instructional design. Plus, many of the bigger companies will have in-house departments that specialize in training and this normally falls under human resources.

It's a good place to be if you like a corporate environment. Most of the work will be for big companies. However, there are some companies that are much smaller and provide training materials to larger companies. There's always going to be a healthy market for writers who can create instructional materials. As a writer/ instructional designer, you're going to have to liaise with a wide variety of people and work successfully with them. You're going to have to be a strong technical writer, and you're also going to have to know how to use various tools including word processing programs, PowerPoint, maybe even video and audio. You're gong to have to learn how to use these particular tools at an advanced level.

How to Break In

Several colleges and universities offer resources and degrees. However, you can join a company and end up in the instructional design department or training department. There are some entry level jobs available in this particular arena. It's highly likely you'll need a college degree. And again, one in a human resources related field would be valuable.

What You Can Expect to Earn

An entry level salary in this field is going to be around $40,000 and somebody who works for 5 years or so in the field can possibly earn $60,000. If you go to work for an instructional design firm, the salaries are going to be comparable. The only real way to make significant money in this field is to start your firm and then to start getting business from large companies.

Street Smart Advice

If you enjoy teaching, if you enjoy writing, if you enjoy the corporate world, then getting into instructional design can be very rewarding. There is always going to be a steady stream of work for the people who can competently produce training materials and related materials.

Additional Resources

1. American Society for Training and Development https://www.td.org/
2. American Society for Training and Development – JOB BOARD https://jobs.td.org/
3. Association for Educational Communications and Technology https://aect.org/
4. Association for Educational Communications and Technology – JOB BOARD https://aect-jobs.careerwebsite.com/
5. International Society for Performance Improvement http://www.ispi.org/

6. International Society for Technology in Education – https://www.iste.org/

7. The Online Learning Consortium https://onlinelearningconsortium.org/

List of Organizations

http://wiu.libguides.com/content.php?pid=73819&sid=844332

OPPORTUNITY #31

Researcher

esearching is, in many ways, the backbone of the writing world. If you're writing any type of factual material or sales material, you're going to need some research. Many writers conduct their own research. However, many writers rely on researchers to help them find the facts. The type of writers who rely on researchers include writers at big newspapers all the way to direct response copywriters who don't want to do their own research or aren't very good at research. Again, very quietly, there's a market out there for researchers. Technically, researchers don't write, which makes researching a good opportunity for people who want to be close to the business, but don't want to be writers full time. It also provides a good opportunity for writers who need additional income while they build up direct income from writing. Researchers can also help with the production of e-Books and materials that are sold online and are a very important part of creating new media.

How to Break In

Even though there isn't as much work in the newspaper business as there used to be, working for a newspaper as a researcher or for a magazine as a researcher can be a good place to start. TV stations will also need researchers and will use interns. The same with radio stations. Internships can often be a good way to begin life as a researcher, plus on many of the websites like Elance, there's also, quite often, a strong need for researchers. Big companies will hire full time researchers. So very quietly, you'll find researchers tucked away within various organizations.

What You Can Expect to Earn

As an intern, the company may not pay you at all or will pay you a very small amount. And in many instances, and in many companies, it may be an hourly position. So, it's not going to provide a huge amount of income. However, it can often provide a useful secondary income or part-time income. But, researchers will typically make around about $20/hr if they're experienced. Researchers in large companies can earn anywhere from $40,000 to over $100,000 depending on seniority and area of specialization.

Street Smart Advice

Once you establish a reputation as a strong researcher, you'll find you can often keep clients for an extended time and that clients will really come to understand your true value. Unless you work in a big company, you're going to have to be aggressive in marketing yourself to organizations and to writers.

Additional Information

Internet Research

Association of Internet Researchers http://aoir.org

The Center for Internet Research http://tcfir.org/

American Writers & Artists, Inc. http://www.awaionline.com/

The Direct Marketing Association http://thedma.org/

Marketing Research

Insights Association http://www.marketingresearch.org

Association for Institutional Research http://www.airweb.org

JOB BOARD http://www.airweb.org/Careers/Pages/default.aspx

American Educational Research Association http://www.aera.net

JOB BOARD https://careers.aera.net/jobs/

Qualitative Research Consultants Association http://qrca.org/

Human Resources Research Organization https://www.humrro.org/corpsite/

Independent JOB BOARDS

National Archives - Independent Researchers Available for Hire http://www.archives.gov/research/hire-help/

SpeechWriting

Professional speakers come in various shapes and sizes. Some are full-time professional speakers who are famous just for being famous. They go to conferences, they speak at seminars, and they will speak to a wide variety of groups. Many of these speakers speak 2-3 times a week and spend almost their entire time on airplanes. Other speakers are often executives for major companies who rise to the top of the company and are asked to make speeches regularly. Then of course, there are politicians who make speeches almost every day if not 2-3 times a day.

Very few speakers write their own speeches. And even fewer make speeches right off the cuff...because that's difficult and dangerous. And so, a big chunk of speakers, whether they are full-time or part-time, rely on speech writers to write their speeches. This provides a healthy opportunity for writers. Speeches don't have to be very complicated, but they need to follow a certain pattern; they do need to be thoroughly researched. Some writers specialize in speech writing and spend a great deal of their time profitably writing speeches.

How to Break In

I think if you meet a speaker, and simply say, "I'm a good writer," that may be enough to get you a job or several jobs writing for a speaker. To break into corporate communications, you'll need to have a degree in a related field... like English. It's an area where it can help to have experience as an intern. It can also be valuable to have written for TV or radio. You can also become a speaker yourself and speak to organizations and use the speeches that you have written for yourself as examples in your portfolio.

What You Can Expect to Earn

If you work in a big company in the corporate communications department, you might be asked to write speeches; it's probably not going to be your full time job, but you will probably be a fairly senior member of a corporate communications team earning about $70,000-100,000 a year. If you're a speech writer for a professional speaker, then you're going to charge probably anywhere from $300-2,000 per speech depending on its length and complexity. A few might hire a full-time speech writer to help them. So, it can be a fairly profitable venture.

Street Smart Advice

It's a field where you need to set your self up as a specialist. Fairly quickly, you can get 4 to 5 good clients. Some professional speakers have huge egos and can be difficult to deal with; they will see you, the speech writer, as a commodity. So you'll have to choose your clients carefully. If you go into politics, you have to understand, it's politics, and that can be a difficult and challenging world. But let's not forget that the President probably has 4 or 5 full time professional speech writers working on speeches. It can also be valuable to have complementary skills such as producing PowerPoint presentations and videos and even audio.

For additional resources and to receive regular updates about opportunities for professional writers, go here (https://www.scottmartincopywriter.com/-for-copywriters-only).

Writing Coach

Many full time professional writers have a writing coach who critiques their work. It's sort of like a professional musician going to see a music teacher or a professional golfer going to see a golf instructor. There aren't a huge number of writing coaches around, but there are some and if you don't want to be in the trenches everyday but still have an interest in writing, then being a writing coach can be a good decision. Many career writing coaches are also career writers. Sort of like a musician who is a part-time musician but also a part-time teacher.

How to Break In

You need to have experience as a writer or an English teacher. The best way to break in is to simply create a website and "hang up your shingle" and say, "Here I am. I am a writing coach." You need to persuade writers that you can provide them with benefits that will really help their career.

What You Can Expect to Earn

Writing coaches can likely earn between $30-70 per hour depending on their experience, their track record, how much business they have, and their level of expertise.

Street Smart Advice

If you're going to be a writing coach, then obviously you need to be a really strong writer. You also need to help your students achieve tangible and measurable results. You're also going to need a really strong web presence. However, this can be a really exciting way to help other writers succeed. Writers who recognize they need help will come back to you time and time again... especially if they see strong results.

Noted copywriter Bob Bly provides numerous resources for writers ... including information about this niche - http://bit.ly/3eaJr2i.

Novelist

M any new writers want to become novelists because it's fun to write fiction. Novelists have been writing novels for centuries, and they'll be writing novels for the next several centuries. There is always going to be a market for fiction, and thus, there is always going to be a need for novelists to write novels. It is a difficult field to break into, as I'll discuss in a minute. However, it's a field where you can almost achieve rock star status. Publishers really need "rock star" novelists. However, hundreds of thousands of writers want to become novelists. So it's a bit of a weird market … a weird arena. If you're thinking about becoming a novelist, it would help to read one of the many excellent books about entering this business. It's a rapidly-changing market.

Start by asking yourself if you want it to be a "one-off" hobby or a serious professional move. If it's a one-off hobby, then I recommend you go through the "print on demand" channel, and there are numerous companies that will print 1 to 10,000 copies of a novel. If you're thinking about making it a profession, then my first advice is "don't quit your day job" and "be extremely patient." I would also recommend you take a quick look at the different categories of novels, because novels come in a wide variety of shapes and sizes.

These include mysteries, westerns, sci-fi, erotica, young adult, romance, literary, and so on. So, think about what really appeals to you and then think about starting off in a category. You also might want to take a look at the top 20 or 25 novels on The New York Times Bestseller list and see what's popular.

Writing novels is one of the most difficult forms of writing...which is ironic because you might think simply making up a story would be easy. You have to make the story believable and entertaining. There's a technique to writing novels, especially when it comes to categories like romance and sci-fi. You also have to develop a specific voice. In many cases, novelists are extremely successful because they create a character, like Harry Potter, and then they build a series of books around that character. James Bond is another example. So, there are opportunities to become a novelist. It's not easy. It never will be easy...even if you're extremely talented.

Fortunately, technology has made it a little bit easier and there are several novelists who have created eBooks and published them through Amazon's Kindle service; these writers have sold tens of thousands, if not hundreds of thousands, of copies. Traditional publishers who publish printed novels look at these novelists very closely and will offer these novelists book-publishing deals. The book publishing world is full of very bright, intelligent people who love books but have no idea how to market. Even if you get a novel published, it can be a frustrating experience getting the book actually sold.

If you're serious about writing fiction for a living, again, there are several books that will tell you precisely how to get started. You really need to read these before embarking on a big career move. Many aspiring novelists spend a small fortune attending a creative writing program either as an undergraduate, as a post graduate, or part time. And there must be hundreds of creative writing programs in the United States and elsewhere. The big problem with these creative writing programs is that they are stocked with failed or semi-failed novelists. So you end up learning from writers who many have had a couple of books published or they may have won a prize that nobody's heard about. They're not really very good, so you end learning from a writer who is poor and it doesn't really help your writing.

If you're serious about fiction, you really need to spend a lot of time reading the very best contemporary and old school fiction. You can often look for 3 or 4 writers you really like and then create your own style by emulating their styles.

In the traditional book publishing world, you're going to need to submit your novel to either a publishing house directly or a literary agent who can represent your book to one of the bigger publishing companies. And it's a very frustrating and depressing process where you are going to hear "no" a great deal before you hear "yes." (If you ever do hear "yes.") So be prepared for a long and arduous road. Every single novelist has had to go down this particular road with a few minor exceptions.

How to Break In

That's a really good question! First of all you have to write a novel and you have to have a good one. Contact the various publishing houses that publish fiction. Many of these publishing houses do not want manuscripts from writers who don't have an agent, so you'll also have to send your novel to agents. There are several books that list publishing houses and several books or websites that list agents. So that's the place to start. If you have some short stories, you can also try to get some of your short stories published in local literary journals. Many literary agents look very closely the work in these literary journals and find writers that way. The other option is to take a creative writing course or degree and, in some instances, you can get referrals to publishing houses and agents. You can also self-publish your novel through print-on-demand or Amazon's Kindle service.

What You Can Expect to Earn

Novelists can earn several million dollars if they become famous and their books are turned into movies. However, most novelists barely earn anything for their work. In some instances, publishing houses will pay significant advances to writers who have proven themselves in the online eBook market. And many novelists have made several hundred thousands of dollars publishing their novels through Amazon Kindle and other online sites. If you want to make big money in writing novels, you've got a better chance of making hundreds of thousands in your state lottery or putting some money on a horse.

Street Smart Advice

There's nothing wrong with being ambitious when it comes to being a novelist, but you also must be realistic and understand that breaking in and being successful is very very difficult. It's best to have another income while you are trying to become a novelist. However, you're going to have a great deal of fun and even if you end up publishing or printing a few copies for a few friends, it can be immensely rewarding.

SEO Writer/Specialist

An SEO writer is a writer who writes articles, website copy, blogs, and other forms of copy with one goal in mind: to help clients rise up in the search engine rankings. The search engines need and want fresh content and reward websites with fresh content by increasing their rankings. This creates a significant market for writers. Content is short, roughly around 500 words per piece, and it typically includes keywords. These keywords are words and phrases that people search for. There is a huge demand for writers who can write SEO content because being 1st, 2nd, or 3rd in the search engine rankings is extremely important for businesses of all sizes. This can be a great way for writers to break into the business as a professional. And you should look at the blogging chapter (Chapter 1) for more detail about one specific type of SEO content... which is a blog.

Many SEO writers are search engine optimization specialists. They market themselves to companies as somebody who can help a company climb the SEO rankings. This can be a rewarding career however you are going to have to learn how Search Engine Optimization works. This can be extremely complex. Search engines also change their algorithms regularly. So in addition to being an SEO writer, you really need to become more than that if you want to make a good living in this field.

How to Break In

Writing the content for Search Engine Optimization is extremely simple. You basically write a 500 word article, blog, or opinion piece and you include keywords. Pretty much any writer with any ability can do it. You can simply say, "Here I am. I am an SEO copywriter!" Within seven days you could be getting work. You'll need to set up a website and you'll need to show people that you can write the type of content they need.

If you want to become an SEO specialist as well, then you'll likely need some training, but if you can execute the techniques, then you can go to a company and say, "I can help you climb the search engine rankings." It helps if you have a track record of success. It also helps if you learn about Search Engine Optimization within an advertising agency or a big company. That can also help you break in if you want to start up your own business.

What You Can Expect to Earn

Many freelance SEO copywriters and specialists charge their clients roughly $400 a month. The pay for SEO articles and blogs can range from $5 to $250 depending on the client and the complexity of the piece. Within a company, if you're an SEO specialist, you can expect to earn roughly $40,000 to $70,000 depending on your level of expertise and knowledge.

Street Smart Advice

It's very important, even early on, to avoid people who are unscrupulous in this particular arena. There are several content-farming companies that will pay $5 an article. You shouldn't accept anything less than $50. However, there is a huge amount of work in this field. And so it's a great place for professional writers to start and earn an income quickly.

Playwright

Playwrights write plays that are performed anywhere from schools, all the way up to regional theaters, all the way up to Broadway, and in other major cities like London. Novelists tend to look down their noses at playwrights as being poor writers, but writing a novel is very different from writing for the stage. Basically, to be a playwright, you have to come up with characters, write a plot, and then put everything together in something that a group of actors can perform.

How to Break In

Some playwrights have agents, but most playwrights have to submit their plays to theater companies in the hope their play gets chosen as one that is going to be performed.

What You Can Expect to Earn

If a play is successful in a major city and runs for months and months and months, you can quickly become a multi-millionaire many times over. One of the excellent things about being a playwright is that you get paid weekly or monthly almost immediately after the play is staged. Of course, 99.9% of playwrights do not make significant money because they are sending their plays to theater groups with tiny budgets. In most cases, the play will only run two or three times. So, it is mostly a labor of love. However, if you do make it big, you'll make it very very big and you'll become one of the highest paid writers anywhere.

Street Smart Advice

In many instances it can help if you are an actor, or even a stage hand, or you are somehow in with the theatrical group in your part of the world. The theatrical community is very tight and almost exclusionary in many areas. You can also go to university to study the art. One of the benefits of going to university and learning to be a playwright is that there is a strong chance, almost a guaranteed chance, that one of your plays will be performed.

Professional Speaker

In the earlier chapter about writing speeches, I mentioned that most professional speakers do not write their own speeches, either because they are not very good at writing or they don't want to spend the time writing, or they don't have the time to do it. For writers who can write speeches, becoming a speaker is a natural progression. And according to an email I just read, there are 7,000 groups a day looking for a speaker. So there's a market for professional speakers. You'll need to have some expertise in your particular field and have some type of selling point that will appeal to a group. I know a professional speaker who speaks about helping young teenage girls make it through their teenage years and she makes a small fortunate speaking. She is on airplanes a great deal and she also has an agent who books her as well, and that helps greatly. However, if you are a writer and you have an area of expertise and you enjoy speaking, and you have something to say, then taking your writing career to the next level and becoming a speaker would be a profitable venture.

How to Break In

You can always go straight to a speaker's bureau and see if they will take you on. You'll have to be fairly well known as a writer or have a very strong area of expertise ... and really be a leader in your field. You can contact groups directly; in even moderately sized cities there are always groups looking for a speaker. At first you may end up speaking to a group of five people in a Denny's at 6:30 in the morning, but at least you are getting started. Once you have some experience, you can start speaking to larger groups.

What You Can Expect to Earn

Once you get onto a fairly decent sized circuit, many professional speakers earn $5,000 a speech, and that's typically at bigger events and conferences. Locally, you can earn $100 to $300 per speech, maybe more. And that can be good extra money if you consider speaking a part time job. And of course, if you are super famous, you can start earning speaking fees of $20,000, $30,000, and even more, per speech.

Street Smart Advice

If you're a good writer, your writing skills will help you become a good speaker. However, many people don't like speaking in front of groups. You're going to have to overcome any fears you have about speaking in public. You're going to have to rehearse. It can help to hire a speaking consultant to help you with your presentation. Because if you're going to be serious about being a writer who is also a speaker, to earn the biggest fees, you're going to have to make sure that you can really put on a show. You may need to hire AV people. You also may need to be very strong when it comes to PowerPoint and other presentation tools. You are also going to spend a great deal of time traveling around the country which of course is a good thing, because that means you are busy and you are earning fees. Many of today's gurus in various fields built their careers and their reputations by speaking regularly at conventions.

Noted copywriter Bob Bly provides numerous resources for writers ... including information about this niche - http://bit.ly/3eaJr2i.

For additional resources and to receive regular updates about opportunities for professional writers, go here (http://bit.ly/3rlChfk).

Magazine Publisher

The person who makes almost all the decisions in a magazine is the publisher. The publisher controls the editorial content, the advertising, circulation, technology, and more. In the bigger publications, the publisher has a team to look after all the work. Of course, it's the publisher's job to choose the people who will perform that work. In many cases, the publisher has been a writer and even continues to write. So there's a significant writing element. The publisher usually has a significant say in the editorial direction of the magazine. Print magazines still flourish and almost all of them have an online presence ... so you'll need to understand the print and online worlds.

How to Break In

You can start your own magazine or you can buy one. That makes you the publisher! In larger publishing companies, you'll need to work your way up the corporate ladder. You can start as a writer. Or you can come up through the advertising or circulation side.

What You Can Expect to Earn

Magazine publishing used to be an extremely profitable business and it remains so for some publications. As the owner, your earnings will vary depending on the profit but margins of 25% were not uncommon. In a larger company, publishers can earn upwards of $150,000 plus bonuses.

Street Smart Advice

Being the publisher of a magazine is stressful. You have to manage several people and the financial pressures can be intense. You'll write some but not as much as you'd like. Today, you must also understand the technology and social media: magazines have expanded well beyond the printed versions. Being a publisher can seem like a glamorous job but there's a reason publishers get paid significant sums. It's almost a round-the-clock-job.

English as a Second Language

There's a significant need for writers in the English as a Second Language industry. You'll have to write learning materials and teach people how to write. So working in this field combines writing with teaching. You don't always have to speak the student's native language but it can help.

One benefit of this field is travel: in many cases, you'll get to live overseas. And today, technology means you can teach students from your living room so you can live pretty much anywhere. Teaching ESL students can be a full-time or part-time gig.

How to Break In

If you're an ESL teacher teaching in Japan, you'll need to speak Japanese, most likely. But it's not essential. Being a teacher can help but again, it's not mandatory. Contact ESL schools directly. You'll find them in most major cities around the world. However, you can teach remotely.

What You Can Expect to Earn

It depends on the location in many cases but you'll earn more than a school teacher...but not by much. If you live overseas, the company may cover most of your expenses.

Street Smart Advice

This can be a fun way to write, teach people to write, and travel. It's not the easiest way to earn a living as the pay will not be excellent. So this corner of the writing world is perhaps best suited for younger writers or the semi-retired.

Writing Video Scripts

Millions of videos are filmed every day. Many of them take place in the corporate environment, especially for training purposes. Some videos are documentaries. Whatever the format and purpose, a writer must write the script. Videos will last from 3 minutes to 2 hours or more depending on the video.

Writing a video script is difficult. You have to understand the goal of the video, communicate effectively, work with the producer, work within a budget, and then help with production. You may even have to narrate the video yourself. The writer is a pivotal part of a successful video.

How to Break In

You can become an intern with a video production company and work with a writer...and learn the trade. You can learn to write scripts in the communications department at a university or college; you can also learn to write scripts through online courses. To build a portfolio, you can create your own videos. Many large corporations have in-house video departments where they need scriptwriters.

What You Can Expect to Earn

A video scriptwriter working in-house can earn from $40,000 a year to upwards of $75,000. It will be the same at an agency or video production company. Freelance script writers can earn significantly more but only if you're busy.

Street Smart Advice

The tough part about writing a video script is the speed of writing. It can take several days just to write a minute of video. It all depends on the complexity and goal of the video. You also have to take into consideration the budget. In many cases, you'll need to attend the shooting and change the script on the fly. However, it can be fun and if you can write solid scripts, there will be a big demand for your services.

Writing Case Studies

A case study is an essay detailing how a company helped a client or customer. For example, a company in the beer dispensing business might produce a case study showing how they helped a restaurant sell more beer to more customers by installing a new beer system. Or a company that sells aircraft equipment can create a case study showing how it helped an airline improve performance and save millions.

Case studies are important because they provide proof the company can do what it promises. Every company needs case studies and a few will realize this; this provides a writer with the opportunity to write these case studies. There are several writers who specialize in writing case studies and this provides a steady stream of freelance work. Writers in large corporations also write case studies as part of their daily work. Writing case studies requires mostly journalistic skills: you're essentially writing an article about the company and its achievements. However, a case study is ultimately an advertisement for the company.

How to Break In

During an internship with a company, you can write case studies and build a portfolio. If you join a company in the communications or PR department as a writer, you will likely write some case studies. Companies and agencies are often looking for writers to write case studies on a freelance basis. If you have experience writing articles, especially business articles, this will often suffice.

What You Can Expect to Earn

Fees for case studies vary depending on the length of the case study and the amount of research needed. Fees can range from $500 to $2,000 and more.

Street Smart Advice

Very quietly, several prosperous freelance writers specialize in writing case studies. It's a little hard to market yourself so you'll need a website that's optimized for SEO. Some companies will need you to travel to gather the information. Writing case studies can be an excellent second career for journalists.

Writing for Radio

What is talk radio? Words. While many stations have talk show hosts who pretty much make it up as they go along, writers have to write ads, write the news, write promos, and write the research. So there's a TON of daily writing at a radio station.

Typically, radio writers are people who love radio. They grew up listening to the radio and always wanted to be part of a station. Many writers perform double duty as DJs, advertising salespeople, and producers.

How to Break In

Because radio is somewhat vocational, it can be tough to break in. Many people start as interns then move up. Some people have university or college training. Most radio stations will have some type of entry-level opportunity, even if it's somewhat menial. But it's a start. If you know how to sell advertising, this can help.

What You Can Expect to Earn

Here's the bad news. Pay in radio is often comically low, unless you're a super-popular morning DJ or you have a massive following plus some syndication. But rank and file writers in radio stations receive very poor pay. You may be able to earn a little more if you also sell advertising.

Street Smart Advice

If you want to be a writer inside a radio station, it helps if you have an additional marketable skill...like being able to produce. Or being a DJ. Still, the pay within a radio station can be poor. So it's important to see your career as somewhat of a vocation.

Writing Copy for Pay Per Click Advertising

As soon as search engines like Google started to take over the planet, advertising changed. Suddenly, these tiny little ads appeared on the search engines and on websites. There are two types of ads in the online world.

Search ads (like the ones you see on Google).

Display ads (like you see on websites and in pop up ads).

These ads provide two sources of work for writers. First, the writer has to write the pay per click (PPC) ads. Then the writer has to write the follow up copy for advertorials and landing pages. These writers mostly follow the principles of direct response copy. The PPC ads need to be catchy and short. The advertorials can be longer; landing pages can be extremely long, depending on the product.

If you're a PPC writer, you can also position yourself as a PPC expert. This makes you more attractive to potential clients. However, becoming a PPC expert is difficult because PPC advertising can be complex. Still, the PPC world provides a steady stream of work for tens of thousands of writers.

How to Break In

You can attend a course in PPC writing and position yourself as a PPC writer. It can be that easy. You can also join an advertising agency and join the digital marketing department. Many big companies keep their PPC in-house. To be effective in this environment, you need direct response writing skills, but you must also understand how to crunch the data.

What You Can Expect to Earn

Some PPC experts make well into six figures. However, most freelancers earn around $50 to $75 an hour. You'll earn $40,000 to $70,000 in an agency as a PPC writer or expert.

Street Smart Advice

Remember that PPC writing is a branch of direct response marketing, whether the PPC people want to admit this or not. You're going to test everything so be flexible, be prepared for failures, and follow the data, not your gut. PPC writing is all about results. You must also understand digital marketing. Still, this field will continue to expand in years to come. If you can produce results, you'll be in great demand. Once you have some know-how and results, you can also teach digital/PPC marketing. Teaching PPC writing can be lucrative.

Noted copywriter Bob Bly provides numerous resources for writers ... including information about this niche - http://bit.ly/3eaJr2i.

The American Writers and Artists Institute (AWAI) provides numerous resources for writers who want to write for this niche. Discover more at their website: www.awaionline.com/go/index.php?af=1578337.

For additional resources and to receive regular updates about opportunities for professional writers, go here (http://bit.ly/3rlChfk).

Writing for eBay and Auction Sites

At any given moment, there are tens of millions of items for sale on eBay and other auction sites. It's estimated there are 110 million items for sale at any given time on eBay alone.

It's PROVEN that strong writing and presentation help to sell more on eBay and auction sites. Several writers specialize in writing eBay descriptions. However, most of these specialists provide the complete suite of services...including listings, shipping, and more. Many retail companies employ a full-time eBay specialist; this person's job will include a lot of writing.

How to Break In

You can gain some experience by selling your own items. You can also buy courses about auction site writing and presentation. Then you're pretty much good to go! You basically show up or hang up your shingle, and get going. So writing for auction sites presents an excellent opportunity for the new writer.

What You Can Expect to Earn

Working for a retailer, you'll earn around $40,000 in salary. You may get a bonus or percentage of the gross. As a freelancer with your own business, you can charge by the listing or earn a retainer. You can also charge a percentage of the sale. Many auction writers specialize in writing for certain segments. Many companies want to get on eBay but just don't have the time. So there's a significant opportunity for writers and auction experts.

Street Smart Advice

To be effective in this space, you must fully understand eBay and how auction sites work. And remember, auction sites regularly change their rules and regulations. It's also vital to understand how direct marketing works... these principles work in the online auction environment. You'll want to provide the full suite of services to be as successful as possible.

Writing Family Histories and Biographies

If you look on Amazon, you'll find hundreds of thousands of family histories and biographies. These have been mostly self-published. Very quietly, there's a huge market for writers to help with these books. And many writers specialize in this field. In addition to writing the book, you'll have to guide the client through the publishing process. This can be difficult but it's part of the gig. Fortunately self-publishing is much easier today due to technology advances.

The process can be long and involved. You'll have to:

- Sell your service to the client.
- Negotiate a price.
- Gather all the information.
- Write the book.
- Create the book.
- Supervise production.

Plus you will likely work with people who are not familiar with the publishing process. It's also a "one and done" business. So you'll have to market yourself and build a strong website.

How to Break In

A few companies specialize in this field but most people use freelancers. It can help if you have experience writing a book. Start by writing and producing your own family history. Then you'll have all the experience you need.

What You Can Expect to Earn

Researching, writing, and producing a book is a monumental task. It takes a huge amount of time, especially if the client is fussy and demanding. So you must price projects accordingly. This can, and should, start at around $25,000 per book. However, you'll find that budgets are usually much less.

Street Smart Advice

Take charge of projects, and always make sure you're in total control. And make sure you charge enough to cover your time. Writing a book is complex and time-consuming. However, this can be a rewarding field once you understand the process. It's also fascinating and you'll meet some amazing people with some amazing stories.

OPPORTUNITY #46

Direct Mail

Some people call it junk mail, but I call it "gold" mail. Those letters and post cards and everything else? They help people make gobs of money. And, of course, writers have to write all this mail.

Yes, much of the mail now comes to you online. So the work has declined a little for direct mail writers. But mail is actually making a comeback. Either way, there's a TON of work available for direct mail writers. However, direct mail writers are not called direct mail writers: they are direct response copywriters.

Writing for the mail differs a little from writing for the web or TV but the principles are essentially the same.

If you're writing a letter, the envelope copy must persuade the reader to open the envelope. Then the words in the letter must persuade the reader to take the next step in the sales process. If you can produce results in direct mail, you'll be in big demand. You're not really a writer, you're a salesperson.

How to Break In

Direct mail companies are always looking for direct response copywriters who can produce results. However, getting experience can be difficult. There isn't a college course that teaches direct response copywriting or writing for direct mail. The key to gaining experience is getting an entry-level position with a direct mail company. Before you start writing direct mail, you must fully understand the techniques. Many companies that provide direct mail services and sell through the mail will train writers.

What You Can Expect to Earn

As an entry-level writer with a direct mail company, you can expect to earn around $40,000 a year. As you start to produce results, you can expect a higher salary. Eventually, you can earn a royalty for each mailing.

Some freelance direct mail copywriters earn over $1 million a year. This comes from fees plus royalties based on sales. So the potential for earning a significant income is very real. But you must be in the top 5% of direct response copywriters.

Street Smart Advice

As it becomes increasingly expensive to acquire customers through the Internet, due to the cost of pay per click advertising, companies are going to rediscover the mail. It's already happening. So there's a huge potential market for direct mail copywriters who can produce results.

However, you must fully understand the techniques that direct mail copywriters use to generate response. Learning these techniques can take 2-3 years.

Noted copywriter Bob Bly provides numerous resources for writers ... including information about this niche - http://bit.ly/3eaJr2i.

The American Writers and Artists Institute (AWAI) provides numerous resources for writers who want to write for this niche. Discover more at their website: www.awaionline.com/go/index.php?af=1578337.

For additional resources and to receive regular updates about opportunities for professional writers, go here (https://www.scottmartincopywriter.com/-for-copywriters-only).

Social Media Writer and Specialist

Social media includes Facebook, Twitter, LinkedIn, Pinterest, and hundreds of other sites. The usual suspects. Many companies and many highly paid social media consultants believe that social media is the "be-all and end-all" of marketing. To wit: we can all go home because social media brings gobs of clients and customers in the door.

Those in other forms of marketing and media will dispute this but the truth remains: social media can be a vital factor in marketing. Personally, I think it's one part of the mix.

However, the foundation of effective social media *is writing*. As a writer, you'll need to create high quality content for social media sites. This can vary from simple Facebook posts to Twitter posts to longer blogs. Again...it all starts with writing.

How to Break In

Because so many companies are coming to realize the importance of social media, new social media jobs are being created every day. Small companies are using social media but massive companies are also in the game.

Here's how to get going.

- Read everything you can about social media.
- Create your own social media presence.
- Learn to use the tools.
- Take on a couple of non-profits to gain additional experience.

You'll quickly have an extensive portfolio you can show to prospective clients or a large company.

What You Can Expect to Earn

An entry-level specialist can earn $35K to $45K a year with a company or advertising agency. As a freelancer, you can earn $200-$500 per client per month. Several high-priced social media consultants earn well into six figures by speaking, selling information products, and providing advice.

Street Smart Advice

Anything you can do to show direct results will help. The person hiring you to take care of social media will often know little or nothing about social media; this can be a blessing and a curse. It's important to understand how to keep people engaged with the content. This means making the content interesting. Again, 70% of your work is writing. The remainder is understanding how to use the technology.

Nonfiction Writer

Look at the New York Times and you'll see a bestseller list for fiction and another for nonfiction. The nonfiction world includes:

- Biographies
- Children's Books
- How To Books
- Guides
- Autobiographies
- Histories
- Sports
- And more

Pretty much any book that isn't fiction. This presents colossal opportunities for writers to write books. Publishers must have books to publish. So they must have authors. You can go the traditional publishing route or you can self-publish or use digital publishing. You can also try publishing "how to" information. More on that in a later chapter. And if writing books isn't for you, you can write nonfiction articles for magazines and websites.

How to Break In

Every year, thousands of new writers get published. Yes, you have to know how to write but the power of the idea is ultimately more important. The key is understanding how the publishing process works. So, before writing a book or an article, take some time to discover the structure. Then take some time to understand the publishing process.

What You Can Expect to Earn

You can earn $50 for a nonfiction article. Or you can earn a $1 million advance for a nonfiction book. The pay for nonfiction varies massively...as you can see. Many nonfiction writers have discovered a way to earn excellent income through Amazon's Kindle platform. I've heard stories of nonfiction writers earning upwards of $300,000 from Kindle books.

Street Smart Advice

Understand how to write an article or book.

Understand how the publishing business works.

Follow your passion. If you like golf, don't write about flowers.

Explore digital publishing and self-publishing.

A physical book can be a great marketing tool for professionals.

If you want to make a big profit writing nonfiction, head for the most profitable categories like weight loss, sex, and money.

Determine why you want to write the book. Money? Prestige? Additional income? Fun?

www.gettingyourbookpublished.com

The "Guru" Industry

Human nature dictates that people like to follow people who are experts. Today, these experts are generally known as "gurus" which can be seen as a somewhat derogatory term.

Perhaps due to the explosion of Internet marketing, the world is full of gurus who speak about anything and everything. They also publish material. You'll find gurus in almost every field and category. At their core, these gurus are information marketers. And information marketers have a huge need for writers. The guru industry needs speechwriters, book writers, editors, and copywriters.

Many writers have become gurus and earn massive fees from speeches, books, referral commissions, plus their own information products.

How to Break In

Establish yourself as an expert. It helps if you ARE an expert but plenty of gurus are not always the best in their field. But don't tell anyone!

Create information products around your expertise. Books, manuals, how-to guides, etc.

Build a strong website that proves you're an expert.

Get out there and speak.

Sell your products in the back of the room and build an email database.

Keep selling products and services to your loyal following.

Provide coaching and/or consulting services.

What You Can Expect to Earn

At first, earning income as an expert can be tough. You're building a business. You may have to speak for free at first then earn income through selling products at the back of the room. However, if you follow the typical path to "guru-dom" and you're successful, you can earn well into six figures. But you must be entrepreneurial. Companies are not going to pay you as a full-time employee.

Street Smart Advice

Some people look down their noses at "gurus" but I admire anyone who has the guts to become one. You'll need to have a thick skin. You must be able to speak. You must be engaging, plus you must be extremely entrepreneurial. You'll likely spend a lot of time on planes. However, if you're successful as a guru, you'll earn significant income. But remember, you'll need to be a great writer...or you'll need to hire one.

Of course, you can also write for the guru industry. Gurus need a ton of writing; gurus need everything from manuals to copy and from emails to brochures.

The American Writers and Artists Institute (AWAI) provides numerous resources for writers who want to write for this niche. Discover more at their website: www.awaionline.com/go/index.php?af=1578337.

For additional resources and to receive regular updates about opportunities for professional writers, go here (http://bit.ly/3rlChfk).

Writing Rap Lyrics

Whether or not you like rap, you have to admit the following: rap has created a lot of work for writers. A rap album might have 10 songs. Each song has around 1,000 words. 10,000 words...all rhyming and in rhythm. Rappers, like most pop stars, need songs and so there's a need for writers who can write songs...but especially for writing rap lyrics. There aren't many company jobs writing rap lyrics so you're going to be an independent operator.

How to Break In

You'll need to meet established and up-and-coming *artistes*. That's up to you. You'll also need to write lyrics and recite them on MP3s and it may help to get on YouTube. It can help if you link up with a musician who writes rap songs but doesn't necessarily like to write the lyrics. You can also use your writing skills to become a rapper.

What You Can Expect to Earn

Several rappers are multi-millionaires. Some write their own lyrics. Some don't. If you write the lyrics for a rap song that becomes a big hit, you can earn tens of thousands in royalties. However, for every rap lyricist that makes millions, there are hundreds who never make a penny.

Street Smart Advice

You must understand the business of writing lyrics and make sure that you have all the legal matters in order...to protect your work.

Songwriting Top Associations:

*** Nashville Songwriters Association International (AKA National Songwriters Association) http://www.nashvillesongwriters.com/

***Songwriters Guild of America http://www.songwritersguild.com/sandboxsga2010/index.html

***American Society of Composers, Authors, and Publishers (ASCAP) http://www.ascap.com/

Top Job Boards

***Songwriters Guild of America – Professional Services http://www.sga-cap.com/services.html

***Nashville Songwriters Association International (AKA National Songwriters Association) http://www.nashvillesongwriters.com/

About

The Nashville Songwriters Association International (NSAI) is the world's largest not-for-profit songwriters trade association. Established in 1967, the membership of more than 5,000 active and pro members spans the United States and six other countries. NSAI is dedicated to protecting the rights of and serving aspiring and professional songwriters in all genres of music.

Mission Statement

The Nashville Songwriters Association International (NSAI) consists of a body of creative minds, including songwriters from all genres of music, professional and amateur, who are committed to protecting the rights and future of the profession of songwriting, and to educate, elevate, and celebrate the songwriter and to act as a unifying force within the music community and the community at large.

***Songwriters Guild of America http://www.songwritersguild.com/sandboxsga2010/index.html

The Songwriters Guild of America is comprised of three entities:

the Songwriters Guild of America (SGA), itself, which offers education, advocacy, services and events to advance the goals of its professional and developing songwriters;

the Songwriters Guild of America Foundation, a non-profit agency that offers services to communities and populations, especially those underserved in the arts, and music, in particular; and

The Songwriters Guild of America Professional Services, including Catalog Administration, Royalty Collection, Copyright Administration and a host of other services designed to ensure that professional songwriters' earnings are protected.

Songwriters Guild of America – Professional Services http://www.sga-cap.com/services.html

Similar to benefits a job board would provide.

***American Society of Composers, Authors, and Publishers http://www.ascap.com/

ASCAP, an organization owned and run by its members, is the leading U.S. Performing Rights Organization representing over 450,000 songwriters, composers and music publishers.

National Music Publisher's Association http://www.nmpa.org/home/index.asp

The National Music Publishers' Association is the largest U.S. music publishing trade association with over 3000 members. Its mission is to protect, promote, and advance the interests of music's creators. The NMPA is the voice of both small and large music publishers, the leading advocate for publishers and their songwriter partners in the nation's capital and in every area where publishers do business. The goal of NMPA is to protect its members' property rights on the legislative, litigation, and regulatory fronts. In this vein, the NMPA continues to represent its members in negotiations to shape the future of the music industry by fostering a business environment that furthers both creative and financial success. The NMPA has remained the most active and vocal proponent for the interests of music publishers in the U.S. and throughout the world, a continuing tradition of which the association is very proud.

Broadcast Music Inc http://www.bmi.com/about/

Broadcast Music, Inc. (BMI) collects license fees on behalf of the more than 550,000 songwriters, composers and music publishers it represents and distributes those fees as royalties to members whose works have been publicly performed.

*

Translator

Technology has taken a lot of work away from translators but for serious translators, there's plenty or work. You'll find translators in the diplomatic world, in the business world, and in the publishing world. In diplomacy, you'll be a "live" translator, or you'll translate official documents. In the corporate world, you'll work with managers and executives, either directly or with documents. International law firms need expert translators. In the publishing world, you'll translate books into different languages. For example, someone has to translate Harry Potter books into Hungarian. And a translator needs to take Hungarian fiction and translate the best novels into English.

How to Break In

If you're from Hungary, you'll need to speak and write in perfect English. If you're a native English speaker, then you'll need to speak and write perfect Hungarian. You'll likely need a degree, perhaps an advanced degree, from a college or university. During your studies, you'll need to prove you can translate at the highest level.

You can decide where you want to use your skills. Then you'll need to contact organizations or companies. Visit company and organization websites and apply directly online.

What You Can Expect to Earn

In a corporate position, you can expect to earn a salary in the $45K to $100K range depending on location. You'll find great jobs in the diplomatic field. Pay will likely be less in the publishing world.

Street Smart Advice

Especially in the publishing world, you'll need to have a good grasp of the nuances of the language. If you like to travel and live in other cultures, head for the diplomatic world. The government jobs can be excellent, with good pay, lots of time off, plus great benefits. A significant amount of your work will be writing-related.

Comedy Writer

The foundation of all comedy is awesome writing. A comedy movie needs a script. A joke has to be written. A sitcom needs writers. Saturday Night Live has a whole gaggle of writers. A play that's a comedy needs a writer. A comedic book must be written. Articles in comedy magazines and and on comedy websites need writers. A show like The Simpsons starts with writing.

If you can make people laugh with your writing, you'll be in great demand. A chunk of the entertainment world revolves around comedy. You'll find comedy everywhere...plays...TV...radio...the Web...clubs...and so on.

The key to being a great comedy writer is a mix of originality, creativity, plus studying the great comedy of the past.

How to Break In

If you're a writer and you can write great comedy, you can choose where you want to specialize. If you want to write jokes, you can contact comedians who will pay for jokes; many stand-up comedians end up in movies and writing for TV shows. If you want to write movie scripts, then it can help to attend a movie program at a university, or you can start to contact movie companies and producers. You can contact local theater groups if you have a play; these groups will often want to give an opportunity to a local writer. To break into TV, you'll need to attend a TV writing course. It can help if you're also a stand-up comedian or actor.

What You Can Expect to Earn

If you write a comedic play for a local theater group, you'll earn a few free tickets or perhaps a portion of the ticket revenues. Stand-up comedians will pay for jokes...but not much. However, if your funny play ends up on Broadway, and is a hit, then you'll earn millions. Some of the top comedy writers for TV earn hundreds of thousands; the top writers for TV shows like The Simpsons can make up to $1 million a season. A writer for a TV show like Late Night with David Letterman will earn $50K to $200K depending on experience. Many sitcom writers are part of The Writers Guild and they have secured significant compensation for their members. Some nonfiction writers who write comedy earn huge advances for their books.

Street Smart Advice

You need to get noticed if you're a comedy writer. Create sketches and post them on YouTube or become a stand-up comedian. Really study the great comedy writers of the past and understand their techniques. Comedy writing often comes down to a mix of topicality and technique. Again...if you can make people laugh with your writing, you'll be in demand somewhere.

OPPORTUNITY #53

Travel Writer

It's a pretty good gig...you travel to a destination that everyone wants to visit. Then you write about it. And you get paid for the "work." You'll find the work of travel writers in books, on the Internet, in newspapers, and in other media, like TV and radio.

Most of the work is writing articles. But many travel writers work on guidebooks and even non-fiction books. Some travel writing is more technical, focusing on travel details and deals. There's a huge demand for travel writing because people like to travel.

Within travel writing, there are several sub-specialties...like writing about golf travel. The Internet has hit the travel writing industry pretty hard; it's easy to find travel information for free online. However, numerous companies still hire travel writers.

How to Break In

The bigger newspapers, magazines, and TV stations hire full-time travel writers. They also hire freelancers. And the smaller newspapers and publications will hire freelancers. Your best bet is to create your own portfolio, or start blogging when you travel. Then you can contact the editors of magazines and newspapers.

What You Can Expect to Earn

Because it's such a wonderful job, competition is pretty fierce. In most cases, the fee will cover your travel. However, full-time travel writers for the bigger newspapers and magazines can earn upwards of $50,000 to $70,000 depending on experience. You'll earn around $400 for a travel article plus expenses. You can earn several thousand for writing a Lonely Planet guide.

Street Smart Advice

If your passion is writing and you love to travel, you can be a travel writer. Either part-time or full-time. If you love travel, you can build your writing skills and the money will help to cover the travel expenses. But it's going to be difficult to earn a solid full-time income as a travel writer. Not impossible, but difficult.

The American Writers and Artists Institute (AWAI) provides numerous resources for writers who want to write for this niche. Discover more at their website: www.awaionline.com/go/index.php?af=1578337.

Screenplays and Scriptwriting

M ovies and TV shows start with a script. In TV, it's a script; in the movies, it's a screenplay. Writers are VITAL to the success of the movie and TV industries. Everything starts with a script.

In TV, you write the script for the show. In the movies, the screenplay is the script for the movie. You work with producers, other writers, directors, and others. You must take a story, or create a story, then write the script. The script or screenplay might not look that complex but it can be difficult. You also have to take into consideration budget, locations, actors, and more; there are lots of moving parts.

How to Break In

Many colleges and universities have film and TV departments; these departments have writing courses. They also have contacts to producers. You can also write scripts and screenplays and submit these to agents, TV companies, and movie producers.

What You Can Expect to Earn

Because it's a unionized environment, writing for TV can be difficult to break into. However, the union has secured high fees for writing TV shows. Many TV writers earn well into six figures; add in residuals, and you can earn well into 7 figures. You can write a movie screenplay and have it go nowhere; you'll get no income. However, the production companies will pay several hundred thousand dollars for a screenplay from a well-known writer with a record of producing results.

Street Smart Advice

If you can break into TV writing, it can be a highly lucrative career. You'll need to get into the union, AKA The Writer's Guild. However, writing screenplays can be highly speculative.

Script/Screenplay Writing Top Associations:

Writer's Guild of America

West - http://www.wga.org/

East - https://www.wgaeast.org/

Top Job Boards

Writer's Guild of America – East – JOB BOARD https://www.wgaeast.org/job-postings/

American Screenwriter's Association – JOB BOARD http://americanscreenwriters.com/category/opportunities/

West - http://www.wga.org/

East - https://www.wgaeast.org/

Writer's Guild of America – East – JOB BOARD http://www.wgaeast.org/index.php?id=53

American Screenwriter's Association http://americanscreen-writers.com/

American Screenwriter's Association – JOB BOARD http://americanscreenwriters.com/category/opportunities/

International Screenwriter's Association http://www.net-workisa.org/

Scriptwriter's Network http://scriptwritersnetwork.com/

Crew-List.net – JOB BOARD http://crew-list.jobamatic. com/a/jbb/find-jobs?oc=6289

Screenwriters Federation of America http://www.screenwriters-federation.org/index.asp

OPPORTUNITY #55

Writing Poetry

Shakespeare, perhaps the god of all writers, was both a playwright and a poet. We'll focus on poetry here. Poets essentially write...well...poems! Poems vary in length and complexity. Some poems are hundreds of pages long. Others are three lines.

Poets are generally extremely serious about their poetry. So it's highly dedicated group. While some countries like the United States and the United Kingdom have a "poet laureate" who is sort of the official poet of the country, the only full-time jobs in poetry are teaching poetry at universities and colleges.

Poets often publish their work in books and online. They also read their poetry at poetry readings. You can earn minor income from getting published either through a publisher or being self-published.

How to Break In

You just need to start writing poetry! To be a full-time poet, you'll need to become a professor at a university or college. This means going through the tenure process.

What You Can Expect to Earn

College and university professors can earn from $60K to $100K. You may get a few copies of the book if you end up being published. But remember that rap lyrics and other lyrics are a form of poetry; there's bigger money in lyrics.

Street Smart Advice

There's a Martin Amis short story where the worlds of the screenplay writer and the poet are switched around. In the story, it's the poets who make Hollywood-type money and the screenplay writers make nothing. That's not reality. Writing poetry is a calling.

Writing White Papers and Special Reports

Companies, institutions, and government agencies regularly pump out white papers and special reports. Companies use them to explain their position or stance on an issue; they also use them as lead-generators. "Give us your information and we'll give you this special report." Some companies sell their white papers and special reports because they believe the information is valuable.

In the government realm, departments and entities love white papers. They hire writers, usually on a full-time basis. Non-profit groups also produce special reports and white papers. Companies will assign their white papers to in-house writers or use freelancers. Government contractors also produce white papers and special reports. In some instances, it can help if you have specialized knowledge. For example, if you have a degree in environmental science, you can write reports for this space.

How to Break In

If you already work for a government agency or some type of institution, you can ask to write special reports and white papers. Interns are often asked to write white papers and special reports. Many advertising agencies will farm out this type of writing to freelancers so check the major job boards.

What You Can Expect to Earn

Governments and companies will often spend tens of thousands paying a consulting firm to produce a study or special report. If you're an in-house writer for a company or agency, you can expect to earn anywhere from $40k to $70k. Freelance rates can vary from $300 to several thousand depending on the complexity of the report.

Street Smart Advice

To get this type of work either on a part-time or full-time basis, it can help if you have secondary skills like creating presentations and publishing. Very quietly, thousands of writers spend significant time and energy creating reports and white papers. And they earn good money.

Writing for Associations

I f you think about it, associations must sell memberships plus they must also communicate extensively with their members. So associations need copy and content. The membership side requires direct response copy that persuades readers to become members. Then the communication side requires content for newsletters, emails, and more. Some associations even produce magazines and regular videos.

Some associations hire full-time writers. Others hire agencies. Some use freelancers on a regular basis. Some associations are non-profit organizations. Others are for-profit. The latter tends to surprise writers. Starting and running a for-profit association can be extremely profitable.

How to Break In

If you have some type of journalistic experience, you can be immensely valuable to an association. Contact local associations for freelance work to get started. You can also request an internship with the communications department of an association. In the for-profit realm, you can contact the association directly. If you're a copywriter, or you want to be one, writing in this space can be especially good: the people who run associations are always looking for people who can help them get more members.

What You Can Expect to Earn

In the non-profit world, pay for writers can be pitiful: you're essentially a volunteer. So it's not a great long-term career move. However, if you're a direct response copywriter who can help for-profit associations gain members, you can earn $5,000 to $10,000 for a sales page. The larger non-profit associations will pay a communications specialist around $50K a year.

Street Smart Advice

If you like writing for this space, you can earn a significant income in the for-profit world. However, you'll need to gain some experience in the non-profit world. Decision makers will pay for copy that helps them gain new members; they pay a lot less to writers who perform the "grunt" work of newsletter writing.

Landing Page Copywriter

A landing page is a page on a website where people land. Yes, that's sounds a bit elementary but let me explain. Companies who want to sell stuff must drive traffic (eyeballs) to web pages. They drive this traffic through a combination of sources. They can use pay per click advertising (like Google AdWords), display advertising, direct mail, radio, newspapers, TV, email, and so on...the landing page is the page where potential customers land after being sent there.

So let's say a company sets up a Google AdWords campaign. When someone clicks on the ad, they land on a certain page. That's a landing page. The goal of a landing page is to encourage the potential customer to take the next step in the sales process. This could be making a phone call or buying a product directly or supplying information.

Landing pages are especially important because they must persuade the reader to take a specific action. The cost of traffic is expensive, so the landing page MUST work if the company is going to get acceptable ROI. Copywriters in the digital realm write a TON of landing pages. And at the more advanced companies and agencies, they are constantly testing their copy to see what works.

Some landing pages are several thousand words long. Others are much shorter...around 300 words. Length and complexity depends mostly on the action requested and the cost of the product or service. A landing page that requests information like an email address, name, and phone number is also called a squeeze page.

How to Break In

To write effective landing pages, you must fully understand direct response copywriting. That's because direct response copywriting principles generate response. Once you understand these principles, you can work for an advertising agency or a company. A good place to start is a digital marketing agency. These agencies create thousands of landing pages for their clients. Once you have some landing pages in your portfolio, you can continue to work in the corporate or agency environment...or become a specialist freelancer.

What You Can Expect to Earn

The key to how much you can earn depends in large part on how well you perform. If you can write landing page copy that persuades people to buy, you become extremely valuable. Freelancers can earn anywhere from $300 to $10,000 for a landing page depending on the complexity of the page and the product. In an agency, you can earn anywhere from $40,000 to $100,000 depending on the agency, your seniority, and your location.

Street Smart Advice

You'll need a thick skin if you're going to be a landing page copywriter. A lot of your copy will fail. But you'll get some winners too. It can help if you understand testing. Some companies will ask you to help with the look of a page...you don't need to be a graphic designer but you need to understand the role that graphics play in landing pages. But the most important skill for a landing page copywriter is to understand the core principles of direct response copy.

Noted copywriter Bob Bly provides numerous resources for writers ... including information about this niche - http://bit.ly/3eaJr2i.

The American Writers and Artists Institute (AWAI) provides numerous resources for writers who want to write for this niche. Discover more at their website: www.awaionline.com/go/index.php?af=1578337.

For additional resources and to receive regular updates about opportunities for professional writers, go here (http://bit.ly/3rlChfk).

Sex Writing

This just in...people are interested, *very* interested in sex. As a result, there's a huge market for writers who can write erotica, and write non-fiction for sex. You might think a sex writer writes stories for pornography. That's one option. Some sex writers write advice columns. Others write medical pieces and conduct medical research into sex issues. Magazines like Cosmopolitan are full of sex journalism. Then you can write novels, short stories, and movie scripts. And then several sex writers write copy to sell sex products. There are plenty of sex-related information products.

If you are interested in writing and sex, then you can earn a living. Again, the world is always going to be interested in sex.

How to Break In

You'll need to choose a category or niche. For example, you can decide to go into advice or magazine writing. Or you can go into commercial markets where companies sell sex items. Once you've decided about the niche you want to enter, start with an internship. For example, you can try to get an internship with a woman's magazine and start to specialize in sex writing. If you want to write books, then you'll need to understand the publishing business. You should start with short stories and start to contact literary magazines that publish erotic fiction. If you have more of scientific bent, you can go through the university and college system to get published.

What You Can Expect to Earn

If you see a person like Dr. Phil as a sex writer, which he is, then you can earn several millions writing about sex. Write a sex poem for a publication will earn you about $10, if you're lucky. A magazine writer for a large magazine like Cosmopolitan will earn $60K to $120K depending on seniority. You can write sex articles for pornographic magazines for around $200 to $300. Erotic novelists will earn an advance of around $2,500 for a novel... plus royalties.

Street Smart Advice

Very quietly, there are thousands of writers who write about sex and earn a solid part-time or full-time income. The key is to choose a niche and then specialize in a field. If you can help companies sell sex products, you'll be in great demand.

OPPORTUNITY #60

Weight Loss Writing

People are always going to be interested in sex...and people are always going to eat more than they should. This means people will always want to lose weight. The weight-loss industry is a massive industry and has a healthy appetite for writing. Go to Amazon and your local bookstore and you'll see hundreds of books about weight loss. Magazines are full of weight-loss tips. Entire TV shows are dedicated to weight loss. Plus companies that sell weight-loss products need copywriters to help them sell the products. There's an academic side as well...academic studies about weight loss and fat.

How to Break In

Choose an area of specialization. You might want to enter journalism and magazine writing. If you're interested in the commercial side of the business, learn how to write copy. Follow the tenure track system if you want to enter the academic side of health/weight loss. There's a huge market for weight-loss books so understand nutrition then create a diet. To write a diet book, it can help if you have a degree in nutrition. There's also plenty of work in the pharmaceutical field.

What You Can Expect to Earn

A company will not hire a diet writer. However, there are plenty of opportunities for freelancers and book writers. Publications will pay around $200 to $500 for diet articles. Copywriters who can help companies sell products will earn the most...unless you publish a blockbuster diet book. You might end up earning up to $70K as a writer for a pharmaceutical company.

Street Smart Advice ... The Skinny (ha!)

It's a huge market and there are plenty of opportunities to write about how to lose weight. You MUST understand nutrition and how to lose weight.

Writing for People
Who Market Events

I f you live in a town or city, your town or city likely has a conference center or a hotel with a large meeting room. That conference center or hotel meeting room is regularly full of meetings and...conferences! People and companies put these meetings and gatherings together. It's a huge business. However, the people who organize conferences and meetings face a massive challenge...getting people to come to the conference or meeting. They rely primarily on a specialist copywriter to fill the room.

That's because people who organize conferences and meetings must send out a blizzard of promotional emails and materials to get people to attend an event. Plus there has to be a website with fresh content. Attending a conference is a huge commitment for the attendee. They have to pay for the admission fee. They have to carve time out of their schedule. They have to pay for a flight. They have to pay for meals. They have to pay for a hotel, and so on...

If a conference takes place in September, the promotion starts in October...the previous year. At the actual conference, the attendees fully expect to have a slew of materials ready and that's even more work for writers. Fortunately, most of the people who run conferences understand they must have really strong writers to help them sell events.

How to Break In

You can work on becoming a copywriter then focus on specializing in this niche. Or you can work for a company that stages events.

What You Can Expect to Earn

If you can help people who run events get people into the events, you'll be extremely valuable. If you write all, or most of the copy, for an event, it will be a ton of work and you should charge up to $25,000 or less...but with a percentage of the profits. In-house, as the copywriter, you'll earn around $50,000 or more if you're especially senior.

Street Smart Advice

You'll need to write a wide range of copy:

- Sales Pages
- Websites
- Emails
- Course materials
- Direct mail
- Social media

The key to selling seats to an event is persistence. You have to pound away and this means a TON of copy. However, several companies are extremely successful in this space. Events and conferences can be extremely profitable. Many conference and event companies have big budgets for writing.

Writing for Sports

People who love sports cannot get enough information about their sport. For example, fantasy football is a billion dollar industry. So there's TONS written about fantasy football. Publishers produce approximately 250 books about golf every year. Like cricket? There are plenty of books written about cricket...it's the same with all sports, 'mainstream' or obscure.

If you have a passion for a particular sport, you can earn a living, even a great one, writing for that niche. You can write about sports as a journalist, how-to writer, blogger, or copywriter...the choice is yours.

How to Break In

A great way to start in sports writing is to set up your own blog. And then get going. Then you can start to contact people who publish sports material. In the commercial world, you can contact companies in your favorite area and offer to write for them. Want to write books? Find publishing companies that specialize in your sport and contact those companies.

What You Can Expect to Earn

If you're a specialist copywriter who can help companies sell products and services related to your sport, you can earn close to six figures every year...

potentially more. Cover a team for a newspaper and you'll earn around $40,000 but probably less. But write for a major publication like Sports Illustrated and you may earn much more. Book fees vary from $3,000 to six figures depending on your ability to sell books and come up with engaging topics.

Street Smart Advice

Become a sports writer and you will hardly ever feel like you're working. You may have to travel a great deal. But be prudent about your career if it's going to be full-time. And if you like to write books, remember that you can self-publish.

Writing for Hobbies and Passions

Let's say you LOVE knitting. Or let's say you LOVE building model airplanes. Or let's say you LOVE photography. In each case, you can earn money writing. EVERY hobby or passion produces a need for information. So let's go back to knitting. You can write books about knitting. You can write advertising copy. Or you can write a blog. Or you can write howto information ... and sell that information. If you love photography and you're a keen hobbyist, think about all the writing you see from day-to-day. You'll see writing on websites. In catalogs. In blogs. And in books. There's writing everywhere for every hobby and passion.

How to Break In

If you have a passion for writing copy then you can contact the companies that sell products in your hobby. If you have information to share, you can write how-to information products and sell these online. You can also contact magazines and online publications in your field. You can start by writing a blog and getting a following.

What You Can Expect to Earn

If you're a specialist copywriter who can help companies sell products and services related to your hobby, you can earn close to six figures every year...

potentially more. Writing for magazines on a full-time basis you'll earn any-where from $30,000 to $100,000 depending on the niche. Book fees vary from $3,000 to six figures depending on the demand for information. You can earn a significant amount selling how-to information.

Street Smart Advice

You can have a lot of fun writing about your hobbies, either part-time or full-time. But you must understand the business side of writing.

Podcasting

Podcasting is simply recording advice and giving it away or selling it. You record your advice, turn the recording into an MP3 and people can listen to the podcast.

Some writers and marketers give their podcasts away in order to sell other products down the line. Others sell their podcasts. Very quietly, podcasting is a big market. Over 60 million people listen to podcasts and podcast spending reached $300 million in 2010, according to copywriter Bob Bly. Many people don't like to read but they will listen to a podcast while they drive or go for a run. Most podcasts are produced by writers.

How to Break In

You'll have to be a freelancer and set up your own business. You can choose a niche then start producing your podcasts. You can podcast about almost every conceivable product. You have to understand the technical details but these are not that complicated. Some writers and marketers use podcasting to produce additional income; others make podcasting their full-time business.

What You Can Expect to Earn

If you have major traffic to your website and you have a big email list, you can sell podcasts for anything from $2 to $25 and more.

Street Smart Advice

To be successful in podcasting, you'll need to:

- Get globs of traffic to your website.
- Build an opt-in email database.
- Create enthralling content.
- Understand all the technical details of producing and distributing podcasts.

However, it can be a lucrative full-time or part-time business.

Writing Short Stories

The short story is vital for most fiction writers because most fiction writers start by writing short stories. It's almost like a rite of passage. (Write of passage?) Short stories come in various shapes and sizes and styles. Some fiction writers only write short stories; others mix short stories with novels. A short story is usually 6 to 25 pages. 25 pages to 100 pages would be a novella.

There's a market for short stories...albeit somewhat limited, with one exception: the market for eBooks on Amazon. Many short story writers are earning significant income through the Kindle platform.

How to Break In

You might want to take some fiction classes at your local community college or you can take a degree in fiction writing as a full-time student. There are hundreds of books available about how to write short fiction. You'll find writer's groups in even the smallest communities. Many communities also have someone who publishes a magazine that includes short stories. You can also "go the whole hog" and take an MFA in creative writing either at the graduate or undergraduate level.

What You Can Expect to Earn

Several decades ago when short stories were more popular, several famous authors published successful books of short stories. Perhaps if you're a well-known novelist, a book of short stories might make some valuable income. However, for beginning writers, a book of short stories must be self-published. So you'll have to market the book yourself. Some publications publish short stories and you'll earn anywhere from $50 to $500 depending on the publication.

Street Smart Advice

You've heard the old cliché, *you have to walk before you can run.* If you're serious about writing full-length fiction and you take classes (or even if you don't) then it's a good idea to start with short stories. However, it's important to understand that you're unlikely to earn serious money writing short stories.

Spiritual Writing

In every country, whatever the most popular religion, spirituality is extremely important. For example, in the United States alone, there are approximately 90 million Roman Catholics. Spiritual writing is a massive, *massive* field with huge potential for professional writers. Here are just a few of the potential categories.

Religious fiction.

Prayer books.

Writing hymns and spiritual music.

Children's books and textbooks.

Religious non-fiction.

Writing for religious publications.

Writing about religion and spirituality for mainstream publications.

Academic publications.

There's a huge thirst for spiritual knowledge and insight. And the people who are interested in religion and spirituality read...so, very quietly, this market is vast.

How to Break In

The first step would be to choose a niche or area of spirituality...based on your area of interest. If you belong to a church, you can visit your gift shop and see who publishes religious material. Contact these publishing companies. You can also start a blog and self-publish your material through Amazon's Kindle platform.

What You Can Expect to Earn

Dan Brown earned several millions from his books, which were based around spirituality (some might disagree). If you become an editor and writer with a religious publisher, you can expect to earn in the region of $40,000...perhaps more. Several religious groups hire full-time writers for their publications and books. If you have a "hit" book based on spirituality, you can earn several hundred thousands.

Street Smart Advice

It's a massive, massive market with many niches. Choose your niche carefully then look closely at who is publishing what; this can be a rewarding area of writing.

Writing Software and HTML

Not all writers write copy, books, articles, scripts, and 'typical' projects. Computer experts are writers, too. And they write the code that makes your computer work.

Software requires thousands of lines of code. And large teams of code writers. And today, the Internet needs writers who can write HTML.

HTML stands for HyperText Markup Language (HTML). HTML must be created so that copy in websites appears correctly when you see it on the web. There are several different 'languages' that website developers use to create web pages. You'll also need to understand Cascading Style Sheets, also known as CSS.

While you're not writing fiction or advertising copy, you're definitely a writer if you write software code or HTML...or both.

How to Break In

It can help to have a degree in computer science. However, ultimately being able to write code is what's really important. You can create your own software and websites to prove you can complete the work. People in this area of writing tend to have a strong aptitude for technology and computers. You can learn code and HTML by attending courses at a university or community college. Or you can take online courses.

What You Can Expect to Earn

There's a massive, massive demand for software developers and website developers. Many companies in the United States and Europe are increasingly looking overseas for this type of work but many still use developers and code writers from within their borders. In the United States, top developers and software writers can earn well over six figures. Some developers work for companies internally. Others work independently as freelancers. There's almost always high paying work for "writers" with this special and specific skill.

Street Smart Advice

Because there's much more demand than supply, there's absolutely no reason to work for a second rate company. Focus on working for the best of the best whether you're looking for full-time employment or want to work on a freelance basis. You should also be able to work from pretty much anywhere.

Writing for Packaging

Go to the supermarket, or the hardware store, or any store for that matter and you'll see packaging. And on the packaging, you'll find a description of the product. In some cases, the product description is long. On others it's short. But there's almost always some type of product description. The intelligent companies make a point to use the copy to sell the product... to persuade the potential buyer to, well, buy.

Many companies create their packaging in house. Other companies hire specialist packaging companies. It's the latter that often hires full-time packaging copywriters. Sometimes the packaging companies hire freelance copywriters who specialize in writing copy for packaging.

How to Break In

It can help to have a background in copywriting. Then you'll want to seek companies that specialize in packaging and related marketing.

What You Can Expect to Earn

As a full-time copywriter for a packaging company, your salary will be in the $40,000 to $70,000 range. Freelance fees will vary from $350 per package to upwards of $2,000 if the packaging is extensive and requires several meetings.

Street Smart Advice

In the next couple of days, pay close attention to the copy on the packages of products in the store. Some copy is dead boring. Some copy enthusiastically sells the product. If you can write copy that helps to sell the product, you'll be in demand.

Writing for Human Resources

A human resources department needs writers...for two reasons. Writing and updating policy and procedure manuals. Writing and creating training materials.

The human resources department may have some additional sundry needs but the primary needs are above. Policy and procedure manuals tell employees essentially what they can and cannot do. Training materials can include manuals, power point materials, and presentations. You can even write video scripts for training.

How to Break In

Some people consider writing for human resources to be technical writing. You can learn technical writing online or through a degree at a college or university. You can start with an internship in a large company's HR department. Or you can work for a consulting company that provides HR services for companies. Once you have experience, you can write for the HR environment on a freelance basis.

What You Can Expect to Earn

As a freelancer, the fee for a large manual or training document can be several thousand dollars. You can expect an hourly rate between $40 to $100. If you work for a company or work for a consulting firm and you specialize in writing HR materials, you can expect a salary of $40K to $75K depending on your experience.

Street Smart Advice

HR departments have a huge need for written materials. You can become a "go to" writer for these materials or you can use your expertise to move up in the HR ranks. You'll need to have a strong working knowledge of the tools of your trade like Word and PowerPoint. The writing isn't always that fascinating but there's a TON of work in this field.

Government Writing

Governments at all levels produce vast quantities of written materials. These include:

White papers

Special reports

Manuals

Training materials

Classified materials

Promotional copy

Policy statements

Laws

Websites

Speeches

And more...

Government at the state, local, and national level hire writers to write the materials they need. Governments also hire independent specialists and firms that specialize in producing documentation. These governments spend hundreds of millions every year on documentation...and thus keep thousands of writers busy.

How to Break In

It can be helpful to choose a niche...or an area of government you find interesting or attractive. For example, if you like politics, you can be a speechwriter for a politician. If you enjoy transportation and public transit, you can write policy documents for a transportation department. You can apply for government writing jobs directly or work for a company that provides the government with documentation services.

What You Can Expect to Earn

While government jobs aren't always the highest paid, the benefits can be tremendous. You can also qualify for a generous government pension. As a writer for a public transport department, you can earn $35K to $50K depending on location. You may find higher pay with the federal government.

Street Smart Advice

Much of the government writing can be somewhat mundane so it's important to follow your passion. For example, if you're interested in environmental issues, you can write about these issues in a state or federal environmental department. If you're interested in aviation, then head for the FAA. You might find higher pay and more variety of work if you work for a company that specializes in providing writing and documentation services for governments.

Marketing Specialist/Consultant

Many copywriters ultimately get fed up with writing copy all the time. So they become marketing specialists or direct marketing consultants. But, in essence, they are still writers. As a marketing consultant, you'll need to write proposals, write marketing plans, help with some copy (in most cases), plus you'll need to speak, write your own speeches, and create presentations. You'll have to write to prove to potential clients that you can actually help them increase revenue. Many successful writers (and many unsuccessful ones) become marketing specialists and consultants.

How to Break In

You'll need to have worked in marketing somewhere...either a marketing department in a large company or in an agency. It can help to have a specialized skill like SEO, PPC, or copywriting. You'll need to show a track record of success. Plus, you'll need a strong network of initial clients. You'll need to market yourself to the target market that will hire you. It could be large companies or it could be small companies in a group setting.

What You Can Expect to Earn

Even as a mid-level marketing consultant, you can earn significant fees...provided you help produce results. Some consultants charge up to $10,000 a day. Some are closer to $30,000. Some consultants speak at events and get a $5,000 to $10,000 fee plus the chance to sell products in the back of the room. Some will charge a fee for ongoing consultation...probably around $200 an hour. So the potential rewards are strong. But your clients will expect you to show significant results.

Street Smart Advice

It's a little like the Wild Wild West out there. One way to start is to speak often in front of large groups. So there will be a lot of time on the road. One key is to develop a strong USP (Unique Selling Proposition) to differentiate yourself from the competition. Having a specific skill you can sell can be a good way to get your foot in the door. It's also vital to have a strong network of potential clients. This area is not for the meek. You'll need a type A personality to succeed.

OPPORTUNITY #72

Environmental Writer

The environment is a huge subject around the planet. Environmental issues are always in the news and this will continue for decades. So...this presents a huge potential opportunity if you're interested in the environment. Some options...

Writing for environmental newspapers and websites.

Writing for news organizations about the environment.

Working for an environmental group as a writer and/or communications specialist.

Writing copy that helps environmental groups raise funds.

Writing books about the environment as an academic.

Writing for government agencies.

Blogging and developing a following.

The above represent just a few of the options available to a writer who wants to write full-time or part-time about environmental issues.

How to Break In

It's important to choose a niche, or a direction, for your career in this field. A great way to start is to begin with an internship with an environmental group. You can also take the more academic route and become an associate professor on a tenure track. Many environmental groups will offer internships. To write about this subject, you'll need to understand it thoroughly so you will also need some type of degree.

What You Can Expect to Earn

The only way to earn significant sums as a writer in this field is to help groups raise funds as a direct response copywriter. As a journalist writing about environmental issues or working for an environmental group, the salaries are going to be close to minimum wage...especially when you consider the hours you may have to work. You may be able to earn upwards of $50,000 writing government documents for a department like the EPA.

Street Smart Advice

If you truly believe in the environmental movement (nothing wrong with that) then writing in this field can be an excellent way to fulfill a personal goal. It can be difficult, though, to earn a significant living.

For additional resources and to receive regular updates about opportunities for professional writers, go here (http://bit.ly/3rlChfk).

Critiquing, Editing, and Preparing Manuscripts

Once a writer has written a book, the manuscript often needs editing, critiquing, and preparation. Many writers are exhausted when they have finished their book and need a second opinion anyway. Writers around the world specialize in this field. You'll need to spend several hours working with a manuscript to fine tune the writing and the presentation. Some publishing houses will hire you to complete this work but most of your clients will be writers; some of these writers have never published a book.

How to Break In

It can help to have worked for a publishing house or newspaper but it's not essential. Many English teachers earn additional income from working with manuscripts. You can build your own website advertising your services. You can contact local writing groups. You can also teach writing at local community colleges and get your name out this way. You might try classified advertising in magazines that cater to writers.

What You Can Expect to Earn

You can charge roughly $500 for a quick read through of a short manuscript. If it's a large book, you can charge up to $15,000 for a complete makeover.

Street Smart Advice

Be careful about what you charge because books can take a huge amount of time to read, digest, and change. Books simply take forever to write and perfect.

Teaching Children How to Write

Yes...you might be thinking, "shouldn't a teacher be doing that?" and you'd certainly be partly correct. However, some children need additional help beyond school to keep up. Some parents believe their children are talented writers and need extra teaching. The remedial side of writing is widespread; helping talented children...not so much.

How to Break In

To teach remedial writing for a private company, you'll need to be a teacher. To teach gifted young writers you'll need to set up a company and advertise to parents. It can be helpful to build a network of teachers who know you provide this service.

What You Can Expect to Earn

As a remedial writing coach for children, you'll earn around $15 an hour. You can perhaps earn more as a writing coach for gifted young writers. It will be difficult to earn a full-time income from this work. It can complement and augment other work.

Street Smart Advice

Take advantage of technology if you want to earn a decent living helping children learn to write. You can expand your reach by using Skype or a similar service.

Writing Corporate Histories

When a large, medium, or even a small company hits a milestone like a 10th, 25th, 50th, or 100th anniversary, a company will often commission a corporate history. This could be in the form of a long article or even a full-on book. Either way, the company will require the services of a writer to write the manuscript or even assemble the entire project from start to finish.

At the very least, you'll need to research the project then write the book and go through the editing process. You may also have to collect photos. Writing a corporate history can be a highly involved...yet rewarding... process.

How to Break In

Most large and mid-sized companies use a company that specializes in creating and publishing corporate histories. So it's best to contact these companies. You'll need a background in journalism and it's best to have a book or two in your portfolio.

What You Can Expect to Earn

For a long article that might appear on a website, you can charge from $2,500 to $5,000. If you're writing a full-on book then you should charge close to $50,000; this sounds like a lot, but writing this type of book often requires major research. Plus there will be several rounds of edits.

Street Smart Advice

Before tackling this type of project, make sure you have the bandwidth. The research can take several months. Then you have to write the book. However, this type of project can be extremely rewarding. You get to know the history of a company and its people. You will often work with senior executives so you must be professional in your approach.

Writing Histories of Clubs and Organizations

Every organization of any stature and size will likely have a birthday. And when that birthday is a big one like a 50th or 100th, many will commission a book or article to celebrate the event. If they decide to commission a book or article, the organization will need a writer. When I say "organization" I mean a charitable organization or a golf club or a yacht club...it could be any type of organization.

The history will require research. Then you'll have to write the book and go through several drafts. Depending on the organization and its politics, the number of drafts could be significant.

How to Break In

Most organizations will contract a company that specializes in writing and publishing club and organizational histories. If you want this type of work, contact one of these companies. The company will want to see that you have a journalism background and it's helpful to have a book on *your* history.

What You Can Expect to Earn

For an article, you might earn up to $5,000 depending on the length. A long and involved book that requires much more work could earn you upwards of $30,000.

Street Smart Advice

Beware of politics when you take on this type of work. You'll have to deal with several people in an organization and they will have different views. So it's best to work with a company that produces these books. An account representative will handle all the hassles. Make sure you clearly define the number of drafts you will produce. Then charge an hourly rate for additional drafts.

Organizing Writing Events and Seminars

Writers want to learn how to write. They also want to learn about being a professional writer. Writers will attend seminars to discover more about:

- Fiction
- Screenwriting
- Technical writing
- Copywriting
- Memoir writing
- Children's writing
- And more...

Most universities that have a creative writing program will organize some type of writing seminar or program during the summer. So you can help to organize the event. You can teach at the event. Or you can be the entrepreneur who puts on the show. There's massive money in this niche. And while many writers will not necessarily travel to a seminar. But many will take a writing seminar online.

How to Break In

If you're an aspiring writer, you can often break into the writing business by getting a job with a company that teaches writing seminars. If you're an accomplished and experienced writer, you can often teach at these events. And if you're especially entrepreneurial, you can stage these events and seminars yourself.

What You Can Expect to Earn

If you work for a company that puts on writing events, you can expect to earn $35,000 to $40,000 a year starting out. As a writer who teaches at one of these events, you can earn $5,000 or more a week. You'll earn more at copywriting events than fiction events. If you're an entrepreneur, you can get 20 people into a room who each pay $3,000 for a week of instruction and you complete the math!

Street Smart Advice

This business is increasingly moving online due to cost and scope considerations. However, several seminars run actual physical events that last several days. Either way, professional and amateur writers are always looking for ways to improve and will invest in their development.

Become a Guru

A "guru" is perhaps a somewhat derogatory term for an "expert" who teaches a specific subject to large groups of people. For example, in the SEO (search engine optimization field) there are several experts who do the following:

- Run seminars
- Consult
- Run book camps
- Write books
- Sell information products
- Instruct small group sessions
- And more

So the "guru" is really, ultimately, in the information marketing business. His or her job is to sell expertise about a specific subject. The "guru" business requires a TON of copy. You can write this yourself or hire a team of writers. However, many writers have become "gurus" because it's a good way to sell the information they write.

How to Break In

The key is to choose an area of expertise, become extremely knowledgeable in that field, then blog, write, and speak. You'll need to build a large database of people who want to know a great deal about your chosen subject. Then you can sell them information.

What You Can Expect to Earn

Some of the biggest gurus on the planet earn several million dollars a year. They also have build large brands and have numerous people working for them. Starting out, you can do well to earn a few hundred dollars for a speaking event. But that's part of building yourself up as a guru.

Street Smart Advice

To build yourself up as a guru, you'll need to be patient as you create your reputation and start to dominate your niche. It can take several years to reach this stage. It's a highly competitive field. To make those millions (and it can happen) you'll need to be a writer, speaker, entrepreneur, sales person, and business owner. However, several gurus are more independent and are one man (or woman) bands who earn a good income writing and speaking about their area of expertise.

Noted copywriter Bob Bly provides numerous resources for writers ... including information about this niche - http://bit.ly/3eaJr2i.

The American Writers and Artists Institute (AWAI) provides numerous resources for writers who want to write for this niche. Discover more at their website: www.awaionline.com/go/index.php?af=1578337.

For additional resources and to receive regular updates about opportunities for professional writers, go here (http://bit.ly/3rlChfk).

Write Greeting Cards

Walk into a supermarket, a book store, or a gift shop and you'll greeting cards for all occasions. Guess what? Someone has to write those cards. This means writing the serious cards for events like funerals. It also means writing funny cards for fun events like birthdays. Yes...you can earn money writing these cards.

Big companies like Hallmark hire full-time and freelance writers. Smaller card companies will likely hire only freelancers. For many writers, writing greeting cards is one of many freelance jobs they have.

How to Break In

Create some "mock" greeting cards then show them to the companies that produce cards. You can also try to get a full-time gig with one of the larger companies.

What You Can Expect to Earn

Greeting card companies are notorious for paying poor rates for greeting cards. However, as a full-time writer who can really produce outstanding cards that sell well, you can earn a sensible full-time income.

Street Smart Advice

Before sending "spec" ideas to the greeting card companies, make sure you have copyright protection. In many cases, it can be a serious advantage to have excellent graphic design and illustration skills so you can provide the total package.

Writing for Dating Sites

No surprise...dating sites are taking over the world. You might like them. Or you might hate them. But they're extremely difficult to ignore... especially if you're single. The core of the dating site is the profile. And the core of the profile is the description. For the record, I rarely visit these sites, but each profile is essentially an advertisement. There's a photo (or several) plus a description. Increasingly, men and women who are serious about online dating will hire a writer to write the profile. The reason? More opportunities to attract potential mates. Essentially, writing for dating sites is a niche for a copywriter.

How to Break In

Go to websites like Craigslist.com, and you'll find people who are advertising for people to write their dating sites profile. Respond to the ad with some examples of profiles you've written. Simply ask some friends to write theirs to get started. You won't need many samples. However, some writers take this niche seriously and have hundreds of examples. If you're one of these writers, then you'll need to set up a website with examples plus you'll need to optimize the site for search terms.

What You Can Expect to Earn

$50 to $150 per profile. Perhaps more if you create the profile from scratch.

Street Smart Advice

Because online dating is this ever-growing beast, and because people want their profile to look and sound superb, there's a potentially big market here. And it's only going to get bigger as people realize that the quality of the writing in the profile can make a big difference when it comes to meeting people. Stress results in your marketing.

Enter Politics

Writing is a massive part of politics. Politicians might not write that much themselves but writing is required for:

- Speeches
- Position documents
- Emails and websites
- Writing laws and regulations
- Legal documents
- Political advertising
- Press releases
- Blogs
- Social media
- Translations
- Articles for newspapers and magazines
- Fundraising letters
- White papers
- Books
- And more

Visit Washington, D.C. or a state capital and you'll find hundreds of writers busily preparing a wide range of documents. If you don't work directly for a politician or a political party then you can write about politics as a journalist or blogger. If you like politics and/or have strong feelings about political issues, you can earn a significant income as a writer in politics.

How to Break In

Many people who enter politics start as an intern with a politician's office. However, several writers make the transition straight to politics. Politicians are often looking for writers...especially the politicians who understand direct response advertising. You can also work for advertising and marketing agencies that specialize in serving the political market.

What You Can Expect to Earn

You might not earn any income as an intern, but it's a way to get started. However, as a writer and communications specialist with a national group, you can expect to earn $35,000 to $80,000 or more depending on seniority and experience. Fundraising letter writers can earn well into six figures. You can expect to earn typical advertising agency rates at the agencies that specialize in this space.

Street Smart Advice

Politics is politics, and you have to expect having to play the game. In certain instances, it can help to have a bit of a ruthless streak. Remember that you need to help the politicians and others reach their goals. In the case of a politician, it's getting elected. In the case of a political party, fundraising is a big part of the equation.

Writing Cartoons, Graphic Novels, and Comic Books

Just about every week there's a comic book convention somewhere. On eBay and similar sites, you'll find thousands of comic books for sale. And in newspapers, you'll find cartoons. Graphic novels have a following. And perhaps you've seen the famous Asterix or Tintin books.

Some writers draw their own cartoons. Others partner with a graphic designer and/or cartoonist. However, the writing aspect is extremely important in cartoons, graphic novels, and comic books.

How to Break In

Publishers are always looking for new talent. The best way to start is to produce some samples of your work. If you're also a talented artist, that will help. If you're not, then you'll need to partner with an artist. Contact the publishers of graphic novels directly through their websites. Cartoons are organized by syndication companies and you can see these companies in your newspaper. You can contact the publishers of comic books directly. All these companies will have guidelines for first-time writers.

What You Can Expect to Earn

Be patient when it comes to getting started as it's difficult to break in. But remember that publishers must have strong writers. Take a look at comics and graphic novels to see how they are structured...there's definitely a template, of sorts. Some publishers hire full-time writers and you can expect to earn $35,000 to $80,000 or more. If you become a star in the business, you can earn well into seven figures. However, many writers in this business love comics and simply want to write in this niche...and make sure you attend all those conferences!

Street Smart Advice

One key to this market is creating a strong character or characters. Think Batman or Dilbert. The character will need to have enough depth to last for decades. It's also important to choose carefully when you work with an illustrator. It's almost like a marriage.

For additional resources and to receive regular updates about opportunities for professional writers, go here (http://bit.ly/3rlChfk).

Writing Romance Novels

Literary types might look down their collective noses at romantic fiction but it's a massive, massive market. According to a group calling itself the Romance Writers of America, here's the actual size:

- Romance fiction generated **$1.438 billion** in sales in 2012.

- Romance was the top-performing category on the best-seller lists in 2012 (across the *NYT*, *USA Today*, and *PW* best-seller lists).

- Romance fiction sales are estimated at **$1.350 billion** for 2013.

- **74.8 million people** read at least one romance novel in 2008. (source: RWA Reader Survey)

So there are millions of people who are interested in romance to the point where they will happily purchase and read romance novels. For many publishers, romance novels present a huge source of constant revenue.

How to Break In

You'll need to take a course in fiction writing. Then you'll need to read several romance novels to understand how they are put together. And yes... there's a formula. You must follow the formula or use a close variation. In such a huge market, publishers are always looking for new talent. Contact the publishers directly. You can also self-publish on Amazon to get started.

What You Can Expect to Earn

By self-publishing on Amazon through their Kindle platform, you can earn a few extra dollars for beer or you can have a smash hit that earns several thousands. If you become a star in the romance novel world, you can earn well into seven figures. But you'll need a huge following. Many romance novelists only earn a few thousand dollars per novel plus the potential for royalties.

Street Smart Advice

You'll need to follow the "typical" template. Plus you'll need to develop really strong characters. Many romance novelists use pen names and write up to 10 novels a year. So it can help to write extremely quickly.

Additional Information

The Romance Writers of America (https://www.rwa.org/).

Science Fiction

From Star Trek to Star Wars, science fiction is a massive market. It's a thriving niche with millions of devoted followers. Many science fiction writers become mainstream. You can write novels plus you can also write short fiction. The market for science fiction is $578.6 million and is expected to grow by 3% according to Simba research. In 2011, there were over 6,300 new science fiction books published. And science fiction books often pop up on the bestseller lists. Many science fiction books become movies and TV shows...and many TV shoes and movies beget science fiction books.

How to Break In

It would help to take some type of fiction course. And make sure you read plenty of science fiction books to see how they're constructed. Several publishers specialize in science fiction, so contact them directly. For short fiction, contact magazines and websites that publish science fiction. Many authors today start on Amazon's Kindle platform. If you're successful here, you will get the attention of the bigger publishers.

What You Can Expect to Earn

Develop a loyal following and get your novel turned into a movie and you're well on your way to seven figures. However, you'll want to be realistic about initial earnings. You might get a small advance of around $2,000 for a first science fiction novel.

Street Smart Advice

Some publishers like their science fiction writers to follow templates. But you can be original. It helps if you develop a repeatable theme that can produce numerous books. You can also create a character and base your books around their adventures.

Additional Information

Science Fiction and Fantasy Writers of America (www.sfwa.org/).

Recipes and Food Writing

You've heard of "foodies" I'm sure. Foodies are people who love food; they visit restaurants and food festivals. Foodies buy books and visit food websites. They cook. And they have a huge thirst for information about food. So this means the publishers who supply this information must hire a small army of writers. And there's plenty of regular work available. Writing about food is a perfect job if you love food. Many writers specialize in writing to sell food and food products.

How to Break In

Start a blog about food and write at least once a week. Then you can contact magazines and food websites. It can help to have an area of specialization like Italian food or vegan cooking. Several publishers specialize in recipe and food books. Contact these publishers directly to submit ideas. And don't forget TV channels that specialize in food and run food pieces.

What You Can Expect to Earn

You can earn $100 to $800 or more for freelance articles in food-oriented magazines. For a first book you might earn a small advance of around $5,000 plus royalties. A celebrity chef might earn several thousand dollars per book.

Street Smart Advice

If you're serious about making huge money in this business, you'll need to become a celebrity. So you'll need to have a TV show, website, plus regular articles in magazines. However, if you're simply interested in writing about your favorite subject then you'll have a lot of fun. But there's no reason you can't make a great living. Again, it can help to specialize.

Additional Information

The Association of Food Journalists (www.afjonline.com/).

Writing Customized Horoscopes

Every day, millions of people read a horoscope. And for many of these people astrology is a huge part of their life. They know their own astrological background plus analyze the star signs of their friends and relatives. Many people specialize in writing customized horoscopes based on a person's birthday and their actual time of birth.

How to Break In

You'll need to understand astrology backwards and forwards. So you'll need to read all the books about the subject and perhaps take some courses. Once you have the knowledge, you can advertise your services locally and also go national or international with a website.

What You Can Expect to Earn

$50 to $250 for a personalized horoscope.

Street Smart Advice

Some people write personalized horoscopes to earn a bit of spare money. However, if you're serious about earning a full-time income, you'll need to set up a website and learn how to generate significant traffic to the site.

Writing Film and TV Reviews

Thousands of movies are made every year and thousands of TV shows are also produced around the world. Viewers want to know what these movies and TV shows are like before they spend time and money viewing. Several writers specialize in writing these reviews. You'll see the main reviews in newspapers and their websites.

How to Break In

It can help to know something about movies or to have worked in this field. But, based on many reviews I read, you don't always need to know anything about film or TV. You can start by writing a blog then showing it to magazine and newspaper editors. But you'll need to get a job, most likely with a newspaper as a journalist then rise to become the film and TV reviewer.

What You Can Expect to Earn

A full-time journalist who reviews TV shows and movies will earn from $30,000 to close to $100,000 depending on location and seniority. You might earn $150 to $300 for a freelance review.

Street Smart Advice

Some film and TV writers write to impress other film and TV writers. Which is annoying. Write for the "average" viewer and your reviews are more likely to resonate. Then you'll get a bigger following.

Writing and Editing Textbooks

According to the National Association of Student Stores, students in America spend an average of $662 on course materials...textbooks. And that's every year. Some textbooks cost around $10. Others are close to $100 or more. So it's a huge market. And it's an important market for publishers: they earn a big chunk of their annual revenue from publishing these textbooks. The margins are also high for these books. Professors often write textbooks but it's not always the case. You can be an expert in a given field and write a textbook. Editors and writers must come in to help the professors and experts and get the book to the press.

How to Break In

If you're a professor or expert, you can contact textbook publishers about their needs. If you're a writer or editor and you can help a publisher produce a textbook, you'll be in relatively high demand. It's not an easy task to create a large textbook that weighs five pounds. If you want to work in this field, you'll need a degree in English plus experience as an editor.

What You Can Expect to Earn

If you get a contract to write a textbook, you can earn anywhere from $5,000 to $30,000 or more depending on the subject matter. As a writer or editor of textbooks, you can earn anywhere from $30,000 to $75,000 depending on seniority. You can earn much more if you become the publisher of a textbook company. Some publishers will hire freelancers for this work.

Street Smart Advice

If you're a professor or expert, getting into the textbook gig can become a useful and valuable sideline. For many editors, being in this field is a career move. However, more and more students and professors are demanding online textbooks so it's valuable to have some online skills.

Teaching Creative Writing

Around the world, millions of people are seriously interested in writing fiction. So there's a significant thirst for knowledge. And this creates work for writers who can teach people how to write fiction. You'll find most fiction courses in community colleges, universities, and colleges. You'll teach students how to write fiction plus how to get published. You'll critique stories and novels and help budding writers. Some creative writing teachers are full-time tenured professors while others are part-time or "adjunct" professors or instructors. For many fiction writers, teaching fiction is their main source of income.

How to Break In

You'll need to be a published author with at least one published work of fiction. In most cases, you'll need an MFA in creative writing or a Masters in English. You don't necessarily need a degree in teaching although that can help.

What You Can Expect to Earn

Teaching a course as an adjunct, you can earn up to $1,500 per course per semester...perhaps more depending on the university or college. As a full-time tenured professor you'll earn anywhere from $45,000 to over $100,000 if there's an endowed professorship.

Street Smart Advice

If you're serious about writing fiction full-time, you can develop some useful contacts if you teach creative writing. However, for second income, it's more valuable to earn money as a waiter. You can also write copy or articles. The pay will be better and you won't have to teach. Admittedly, many fiction writers really enjoy teaching fiction writing.

I see the creative writing "industry" as a total scam. You get writers who can't make it as full-time writers (because they're not good enough) teaching budding writers how to write. An MFA stands for Master of F*ck All. Still, it's great money for the universities and colleges that run these scams.

Writing Young Adult Fiction

Young adult fiction essentially targets teenagers or pre-teens. Ages 11-18 approximately. And it's an important niche for publishers and authors. There's a huge school market, but it's the time when children leave "kids" books and start to reader "heavier" material. Some have described the Harry Potter books as young adult fiction.

How to Break In

As with all fiction writing, it helps to take a course in creative writing so you understand the fundamentals. You can take this course at a community college, a university, or online. You should also read books about fiction and writing for the young adult (YA) market. Read several of the top books in this market. Once you have a book, you can contact publishers directly. Today, most YA writers start by publishing on Kindle, which is Amazon's online self-publishing service.

What You Can Expect to Earn

If you only sell a few books to friends through Kindle or self-publishing, you'll earn a few hundred dollars...if that. However, there are plenty of stories about YA authors making it big through Amazon's Kindle...and selling thousands of books at around $7 a book. This can add up to a six figure income just from writing YA books. If you become a famous author and your books make it into schools, you can earn deep into six figures. But it's rare to make a massive income from this niche.

Street Smart Advice

While some YA books are unique and highly different, many YA books follow a formula. You'll need to follow one of the formulas ... at first. You won't want to be too literary in this niche. Keep the writing, plots, and characterization mostly fairly simple.

Headline Writer

It's admittedly an extremely small niche but some of the bigger newspapers and magazines hire writers who primarily write the headlines. You might have other writing responsibilities but many publishers take their headlines, and headline writers, extremely seriously. Have you seen Cosmopolitan Magazine? I'm told the magazine hires highly specialized headline writers for the cover headlines. Headlines are extremely important because headlines sell magazines and keep people reading. Tabloids also look for strong headline writers.

How to Break In

Many headline writers have degrees in English or journalism. However, it's not mandatory. You can start with a relatively basic editing job at newspaper or magazine and learn the art and craft of writing powerful headlines. However, if you believe you have what it takes to write headlines, you can write some "spec" headlines and show them to editors and publishers.

What You Can Expect to Earn

At a writing conference, I heard that headline writers for major magazines can earn $1 million a year. That seems a bit far-fetched. At a major magazine, you'll earn around $100,000 if you're experienced and really brilliant. But you'll have other responsibilities. At a tabloid, you'll earn a little less.

Street Smart Advice

The top headlines are somewhat formulaic. You have to have a strong sense of humor and apply the formulas to the stories. In the tabloid environment, you have to be especially outrageous.

For additional resources and to receive regular updates about opportunities for professional writers, go here (http://bit.ly/3rlChfk).

Writing for Alternative Health

While most people trust their doctor and modern medicine, there are millions in the United States and elsewhere who are extremely interested in alternative health. This can range from yoga to eating a diet consisting of only raw food. Increasingly, people are seeking alternatives to modern food and modern medicine.

This means there's a growing market for alternative foods and alternative health products and services. So this means there's work for writers who can write about alternative health. There's also a market for writers who can help to sell alternative health products. You can write advertising copy, articles for magazines, blogs, books, and more. There are significant opportunities in this niche.

How to Break In

You'll need to have some specialist knowledge in this area. For example, it can help if you understand vegetarian and vegan diets. Or perhaps you're an expert in Pilates. Then you can decide which area of writing you want to enter. Do you want to write for magazines? Or write copy? If it's the former, contact the editors of alternative health publications. If it's the latter, contact companies that sell alternative health products and foods. Several direct response copywriters specialize in writing for dietary supplements.

What You Can Expect to Earn

Write a blog for a news site and you can earn $50 to $100 a blog. However, you can earn up to $800 for a feature article for a major publication. As a copywriter who specializes in this field, you can earn upwards of $2,000 for a long-form sales page and earn some royalties. Many magazines hire full-time writers and you'll earn around $40,000 a year...or more. Some companies hire full-time copywriters.

Street Smart Advice

Very quietly, there are several writers earning valuable six-figure income in this niche. And it's definitely growing as the baby boomers continue to look for alternatives to modern medicine...which is expensive and based on chemicals. But it's vital to understand this niche. You can't fake the knowledge.

Real Estate Writer

A real estate professional once told me that real estate is the largest industry in the world. And it's tough to disagree. The industry presents a deep well of work for many types of writers.

- Editors
- Feature writers
- Authors
- Journalists
- Copywriters
- Bloggers
- Researchers
- Social media specialists.

People in the real estate world have a massive thirst for information. They need data. Plus they need information about excelling in this highly competitive field. Some real estate companies companies believe strongly in communicating and selling and this presents opportunities for copywriters who specialize in real estate writing.

How to Break In

If you want to become a real estate writer, it can help to have experience in the field. You can contact publications about writing real estate pieces. You can also contact real estate companies about helping them with their communications needs. And if you can help companies sell real estate, you'll be extremely popular.

What You Can Expect to Earn

A company might pay a social media specialist around $300 a month to maintain social media...increasingly important in today's industry. As a real estate writer for a magazine or newspaper, you'll earn anywhere from $35,000 to $70,000 depending on the market and your experience.

Street Smart Advice

The big money in this market is in selling information to ambitious real estate professionals. If you can write copy that sells products and services to this market, you'll earn a significant income. However, you earn a decent salary as a real estate specialist in this market...writing for newspapers and magazines.

Fantasy Sports Writer

Fifteen years ago, fantasy sports was a few people in the office organizing a rotisserie baseball league. Today, fantasy football alone is a billion dollar industry...and it's growing. As a direct result, there's work for writers. Why? Because there's a huge thirst for information. In this market, you'll find journalists and copywriters. Journalists provide the information. Copywriters sell the products and services in this rapidly-growing market.

How to Break In

If you love fantasy sports, there's a spot for you in this niche. Start a blog to show you have the knowledge then contact the companies that publish fantasy sports information. If you want to go it alone, find a way to get on the radio...specifically sports talk radio. Major companies like ESPN also hire fantasy sports specialists. If you want to sell products and services, contact publishers and websites. You'll need some copywriting experience.

What You Can Expect to Earn

Earnings vary significantly in this market. As a staffer for a company like ESPN, you can start at around $35,000 a year. Perhaps a little more. As a big name with a big following, you can earn just over six figures. As a copywriter selling services for this niche, you can earn anywhere from $850 and above for a sales page.

Street Smart Advice

You'll need to specialize in a fantasy sport. The two biggest sports in the USA are football and baseball. The big money is in providing information and selling fantasy services.

Gossip OMG!

Open any tabloid anywhere in the world and you'll see a gossip column. In fact, tabloids essentially revolve around gossip. You'll see gossip shows on TV. And most tabloids (and even the 'important' newspapers) will include plenty of gossip. And there are websites like TMZ that specialize in celebrity gossip. The world's appetite for this type of news seems insatiable and, of course, that means writers must report and write. And let's not forget magazines like People and The National Enquirer. Love them or hate them, they need writers. And lots of them.

How to Break In

It will help to have some experience working for a newspaper before venturing into the world of gossip. You'll need to start by contacting the websites, newspapers, and magazines that print gossip. Some writers operate like paparazzi only without the cameras. They write about celebrities then sell the stories on a freelance basis. An internship with a news organization that specializes in gossip can help.

What You Can Expect to Earn

If you have an exclusive on a big story, you can earn perhaps $2,000 for a good gossip story, especially if you have a photo or two. As a gossip "beat" writer for a newspaper, you'll earn $35,000 to $70,000 depending on the location. As a TV writer, you'll earn about the same. Some writers for magazines like The National Enquirer can earn much more. These tabloids are always looking for talent.

Street Smart Advice

Gossip writing is the Wild Wild West of writing world so be prepared. But if you like the whole celebrity culture, then it's a fun way to make a living as a writer. It's not necessarily a growing niche but it's never going away.

Wine and Drink Writer

Among people who like the finer things in life, wine is extremely popular. And wine drinkers are always looking for information...especially if they're really, really into their wine. It's not a huge market but it's a good fit if you enjoy food. There's some writing out there about drink but it's a much smaller market. There are plenty of magazines about wine but I don't remember seeing one about absinthe. There's a small market for wine books. With the rise in craft brewing, there's a small market for beer writing.

How to Break In

You'll need to know a TON about wine and/or drink. You can start your own blog and then show the work to the publishers of magazines that write about wine. Several websites also specialize in wine news. Some wine writers write for mainstream magazines.

What You Can Expect to Earn

As a staffer for a wine magazine, you'll earn anywhere from $25,000 to $75,000. You'll earn more as a senior editor. There isn't much work out there for copywriters who write about wine. You'll earn around $300 to $600 for freelance articles.

Street Smart Advice

There aren't many writers who specialize in wine writing but if you break in, you'll have a wonderful time...especially if you love wine.

Writing Restaurant Reviews

At newspapers around the world, one of the plum jobs is being the restaurant critic. You get to visit wonderful restaurants then write about them. You become a celebrity. Here's a slight problem, though. The Internet is now full of "user generated copy" and this means that everyone is now a restaurant reviewer. If you feel so moved, you can write restaurant reviews yourself and publish a blog.

How to Break In

Magazines and newspapers still employ full-time restaurant reviewers. You'll need to know something about food although it's not vital. Most restaurant critics moved up through the ranks in the newspaper industry.

What You Can Expect to Earn

As a freelancer, you'll get anywhere from $50 to $150 for a review...plus a free meal! As a restaurant critic at a newspaper, you'll earn around $40,000 to $60,000 depending on location.

Street Smart Advice

It's such a popular gig that it's tough to break in. Restaurant critics tend to keep their jobs for a long time...and watch their weight. However, you can bypass the whole newspaper gig by becoming a popular blogger in your city. Some writers and editors help to produce restaurant guidebooks. But even in this market, the content often comes from surveys.

Real Estate Appraiser

In every city and town on the planet, almost, there's a real estate appraiser. A real estate appraiser determines the value of commercial or residential properties. Banks, lawyers, and others can then make decisions based on the value. You might think it's a technical position but, as one appraiser told me, an appraiser is a writer. The result of the appraisal is a long report. Yes, there's some maths involved but, in the end, it's a job for a highly specialized writer.

How to Break In

It can help to have an accounting background but it's not vital. Appraisal firms often bring on trainees to tackle some of the easier work. Then you can work your way up to becoming fully licensed.

What You Can Expect to Earn

Most appraisal firms comprise the owner of the firm plus some associates who are essentially freelancers. The owner of the firm keeps half the fee while the associate keeps the other half. This could produce around $1,500 for a basic commercial appraisal. Some major appraisals produce fees of more than $10,000. It will take a while to gain the expertise and experience to tackle the bigger jobs. You must have a license to be an appraiser so there's a barrier to entry. This helps to keep prices somewhat higher.

Street Smart Advice

If you enjoy the real estate world and you're good with numbers, you might enjoy being a real estate appraiser. However, it's laborious work. On the other hand, there's a constant need for this work so it can be a steady gig. The key is being the 'main man' in the firm so that others are working for you.

Business Appraiser

What's a business worth? That's an important question, especially if you're selling a business or buying a business. If you need to know the value of a business, you turn to a business appraiser. The business appraiser looks at the books of a business and determines its value. Like real estate appraising, business appraising is somewhat technical, but ultimately, it's about producing a report and this means a ton of writing.

How to Break In

You'll need an accounting background. And you'll need to start as an associate of a business appraiser so you understand the trade.

What You Can Expect to Earn

Most business appraisal firms comprise the main appraiser plus some associates who are freelancers. The owner of the firm gets a percentage of the fee. The associates then get a percentage. Fees vary from $5,000 for a simple business to several hundred thousand for a more complex firm.

Street Smart Advice

If you like the business environment and you have a penchant for numbers, you'll enjoy the world of business appraising.

Writing Information Products

The information marketing industry is massive. It's a quiet industry because most of the business takes place over the Internet and through the mail. Information marketers must have their products to sell. And the information products require a TON of writing. Some information products are short and have a low price. Others require a monthly fee. Some have extremely high prices. Either way, the products often include several thousand words. Many are book length. So there's a vast amount of work producing and writing the information products that information marketers sell.

How to Break In

It can be helpful to have experience producing manuals and writing books. You'll need some editing and layout skills. You can contact information marketers directly, usually through their websites. Very quietly, this presents a great way for professional writers to break into the business.

What You Can Expect to Earn

Some information marketers are so large they hire full-time writers to research and create the products. Others use freelancers. As a full-time employee, you can expect to earn around $35K to $70K a year. Freelance fees vary based on the product and how much research you need to conduct. But if you're writing a manual that's 300 pages, the fee can be upwards of $10,000.

Street Smart Advice

As I wrote earlier, there are several professional and reputable information marketing companies. But there are some scallywags in this business, and you need to be careful about payment and terms. It can be helpful if you provide additional services such as copywriting, editing, and layout.

Noted copywriter Bob Bly provides numerous resources for writers ... including information about this niche - http://bit.ly/3eaJr2i.

Writing Your Own Blog

Yes ... you can write blogs for other companies and websites. But many writers make a big income writing their own blog. Others maintain numerous blogs. Here's how it works. You set up a blog, optimize it for SEO purposes, start to build an audience, place ads and affiliate links on the blog, then collect revenue. They key is traffic. When you have big traffic, you can generate big revenue.

How to Break In

It can be really, really easy to start. You just start a blog using one of the many platforms available. These platforms are mostly intuitive but they also provide easy-to-understand directions. You must also have a popular subject in mind.

What You Can Expect to Earn

At first, you can earn a $100 to $300 a month ... if you do well. However, several bloggers earn well into six figures. But you'll have to dedicate hundreds of hours of time before you reach this level ... but it's achievable.

Street Smart Advice

Many copywriters get into blogging as a sideline ... then turn this into a full-time gig. There are plenty of resources available to show you how to turn a blog into money.

Production Editing Assistant

Television production companies and related firms must have experienced writers to handle media management. You'll write content for live events plus manage a database of content before, during, and after the event. You must provide information to be used during the production.

How to Break In

You'll need to develop the skills necessary. Contact a local television company to see if you can intern. Some broadcasting schools teach this skill.

What You Can Expect to Earn

As a full-time employee with a major network, you can expect to earn around $50,000 ... perhaps more. But most of these gigs are freelance and the fee will start at around $300 a day plus travel expenses.

Street Smart Advice

For sports events on television, most of the crew are working with cameras and set up. You will also see the commentators. But writers are an essential resource because they provide background information for the commentators. You will have to travel a great deal but if you get into this field, it can be exciting ... even if the hours are long. It's a growing field because of the growth in televised sports events.

Community Forum Manager
... or Contributor

I f you're breathing, you have likely visited an online forum. You'll find forums built around just about any subject under the sun. From football to knitting and from commercial aviation to cars.

These forums are extremely popular ... even if the user-generated content is not always "totally" accurate.

You'll find three opportunities here. You can set up your own forum. You can manage a forum for someone else. Or you can contribute to forums and be paid for this work. The latter can be a bit of a "dark art" where you pose as a "regular" visitor but you're there to promote a certain product or service.

How to Break In

PR companies sometimes hire writers to post on forums. You can set up your own forum then drive traffic to the site. Or someone who owns a forum might hire you to manage the site. You earn money through a forum by attracting traffic then getting affiliate income.

What You Can Expect to Earn

Many forum sites have become a decent-size business. Others are more of a hobby. Some sites have full-time employees who monitor forums while others rely on volunteers. Working for a PR firm and posting on forums and other social media, you can expect to earn around $35,000 on a salary ... perhaps more. An hourly rate would be around $15 to $25 per hour.

Street Smart Advice

Forums are the Wild Wild West of the Internet. Anything can happen. and people can get away with saying pretty much anything. This presents a huge opportunity for writers ... professional or otherwise.

Curriculum Writer

At schools and universities around the world, coursework starts with the curriculum. Professors sometimes create these but many times, they outsource this work to others in the department or *outside* the department.

Essentially you need to liaise with the academics and others ... and write the curriculum for courses.

How to Break In

You don't need to be a professor (tenured or otherwise) and this can be an excellent part-time job for students.

What You Can Expect to Earn

About $10-$20 an hour depending on location.

Street Smart Advice

It's unlikely there's enough work here for a full-time work but curriculum writing can provide useful part-time income. Some schools at the elementary, middle, and high school level will need curriculum writers. Some school systems hire full-time writers for this work.

Final Words

As I wrote in the introduction, being a professional writer can be an excellent way to earn a solid, even spectacular, full-time or part-time income. It's important to avoid the industries the Internet has hit the hardest ... like newspapers. However, the Internet has, and will continue to provide, huge amounts of work for writers.

About the Author

Scott Martin was born in the United States but spent his formative years in Canada and England, where he attended Harrow School. He graduated from The University of North Carolina at Chapel Hill with a degree in English and Comparative Literature. He was a John Motley Morehead Scholar.

After a somewhat peripatetic career in copywriting, business journalism, magazine publishing, and corporate communications, Scott eventually settled into direct response copywriting and the occasional book ... like this one. Scott's bibliography includes a book about Caddyshack. Learn more at www.scottmartincopywriter.com.

About the Editor

opywriter Christy Goldfeder edited and contributed to this book. Her love of world travel started as a high school junior when she attended School Year Abroad in France. She graduated from Barnard College, Columbia University with a degree in English Literature.

Christy started her career as an editor at the Wall Street Journal Online. From there, she managed content and copy at Madison Avenue marketing communications agencies until transitioning into direct response copywriting. You can learn more at www.christygoldfeder.com

Made in the USA
Coppell, TX
11 May 2022

77673930R00152